D1564835

The Kentucky Bicentennial Bookshelf
Sponsored by

KENTUCKY HISTORICAL EVENTS CELEBRATION COMMISSION
KENTUCKY FEDERATION OF WOMEN'S CLUBS

and Contributing Sponsors

AMERICAN FEDERAL SAVINGS & LOAN ASSOCIATION
ARMCO STEEL CORPORATION, ASHLAND WORKS
A. ARNOLD & SON TRANSFER & STORAGE CO., INC. / ASHLAND OIL, INC.
BAILEY MINING COMPANY, BYPRO, KENTUCKY / BEGLEY DRUG COMPANY
J. WINSTON COLEMAN, JR. / CONVENIENT INDUSTRIES OF AMERICA, INC.
IN MEMORY OF MR. AND MRS. J. SHERMAN COOPER BY THEIR CHILDREN
CORNING GLASS WORKS FOUNDATION / MRS. CLORA CORRELL
THE COURIER-JOURNAL AND THE LOUISVILLE TIMES
COVINGTON TRUST & BANKING COMPANY
MR. AND MRS. GEORGE P. CROUNSE / GEORGE E. EVANS, JR.
FARMERS BANK & CAPITAL TRUST COMPANY / FISHER-PRICE TOYS, MURRAY
MARY PAULINE FOX, M.D., IN HONOR OF CHLOE GIFFORD
MARY A. HALL, M.D., IN HONOR OF PAT LEE,
JANICE HALL & AND MARY ANN FAULKNER
OSCAR HORNSBY INC. / OFFICE PRODUCTS DIVISION IBM CORPORATION
JERRY'S RESTAURANTS / ROBERT B. JEWELL
LEE S. JONES / KENTUCKIANA GIRL SCOUT COUNCIL
KENTUCKY BANKERS ASSOCIATION / KENTUCKY COAL ASSOCIATION, INC.
THE KENTUCKY JOCKEY CLUB, INC. / THE LEXINGTON WOMAN'S CLUB
LINCOLN INCOME LIFE INSURANCE COMPANY
LORILLARD A DIVISION OF LOEW'S THEATRES, INC.
METROPOLITAN WOMAN'S CLUB OF LEXINGTON / BETTY HAGGIN MOLLOY
MUTUAL FEDERAL SAVINGS & LOAN ASSOCIATION
NATIONAL INDUSTRIES, INC. / RAND MCNALLY & COMPANY
PHILIP MORRIS, INCORPORATED / MRS. VICTOR SAMS
SHELL OIL COMPANY, LOUISVILLE
SOUTH CENTRAL BELL TELEPHONE COMPANY
SOUTHERN BELLE DAIRY CO. INC.
STANDARD OIL COMPANY (KENTUCKY)
STANDARD PRINTING CO., H. M. KESSLER, PRESIDENT
STATE BANK & TRUST COMPANY, RICHMOND
THOMAS INDUSTRIES INC. / TIP TOP COAL CO., INC.
MARY L. WISS, M.D. / YOUNGER WOMAN'S CLUB OF ST. MATTHEWS

Dear Alben

Mr. Barkley of Kentucky

JAMES K. LIBBEY

THE UNIVERSITY PRESS OF KENTUCKY

Photographs courtesy of Special Collections,
University of Kentucky, and used with the
permission of Mr. David M. Barkley.

Research for The Kentucky Bicentennial Bookshelf
is assisted by a grant from the
National Endowment for the Humanities.
Views expressed in the Bookshelf do not
necessarily represent those of the Endowment.

Library of Congress Cataloging in Publication Data

Libbey, James K
    Dear Alben.

    (The Kentucky Bicentennial bookshelf)
    Bibliography: p.
    1. Barkley, Alben William, 1877-1956. 2. Legis-
lators—United States—Biography. 3. United States.
Congress—Biography. 4. Vice-Presidents—United
States—Biography. 5. United States—Politics and
government—1901-1953. I. Title. II. Series.
E748.B318L5   973.918'092'4 [B]   78-57391
ISBN 0-8131-0238-3

Scholarly publisher for the Commonwealth,
serving Berea College, Centre College of Kentucky,
Eastern Kentucky University, The Filson Club,
Georgetown College, Kentucky Historical Society,
Kentucky State University, Morehead State University,
Murray State University, Northern Kentucky University,
Transylvania University, University of Kentucky,
University of Louisville, and Western Kentucky University.

Editorial and Sales Offices: Lexington, Kentucky 40506

Contents

To Joyce's in-laws:
Russell and Narcissa

Acknowledgments

QUITE POSSIBLY A hundred or more individuals contributed directly or indirectly to the completion of this project. Alben W. Barkley's long and eventful life required commensurate amounts of time and work in order to telescope the broad sweep of his career into a biographical essay of such a relatively short length. While I must assume final responsibility for the manuscript, my efforts alone might not have reduced such a huge task to manageable proportions without the able assistance of grammarians, historians, and student workers who corrected, checked, or somehow helped me prepare the material presented in the following pages. If I were a wealthy man, more than my thanks would be extended to David Allen, Department of English, George Rogers Clark High School; Charlene Arnold, student, Eastern Kentucky University; Dorothy Bayer, Richmond, Kentucky; Terry Birdwhistell, Special Collections, University of Kentucky; Dr. Harry Brown, Department of English, Eastern Kentucky University; Becky Courtney, student, Eastern Kentucky University; Terry Culross, Department of Learning Skills, Eastern Kentucky University; Ronald Harrod, student, Eastern Kentucky University; Dr. Holman Hamilton, Professor Emeritus of History, University of Kentucky; Charles Hay, Archives, Eastern Kentucky University; Dr. Keith Heim, Special Collections, Murray State University; Dr. Robert Ireland, Department of History, University of Kentucky; Dr. Quentin Keen, Department of History, Eastern Kentucky University; Jacqueline Maki, Department of Learning Skills, Eastern Kentucky University; William Marshall, Special Collections, University of Kentucky; Dr. George Robinson, Department of History, Eastern Kentucky University; Dr. Charles Roland, Department of History, University of Kentucky; Dr. Charles Talbert, Professor Emeritus of History, University of Kentucky; James Tatum, student, Eastern Kentucky University; Terry Warth, Special Collections, University of Kentucky. Two individuals deserve a special word of thanks. My wife, Joyce, and Dr. James Klotter, Kentucky Historical Society, read the entire manuscript and gave me the type of encouragement and support that can only be compensated with my eternal gratitude. Finally, I must mention my peripatetic colleague, Professor Ann Algier, whose Renaissance mind gives her the special grace it takes to inspire confidence and create worth in every imaginable intellectual endeavor, including this biography.

It would be fruitless and possibly embarrassing in my neglect to credit the numerous Barkley buffs, friends, or relatives who shared with me their impressions. None, though, were more helpful or important than the comments I received through interview or correspondence with Alben's children: David Barkley, Laura MacArthur, Marian Truitt. Mr. Barkley generously allowed me to rummage about the Angles estate in order to acquire the flavor of his father's last home. In addition, and despite his illness, David Barkley continued to express his warm interest and give me his kind aid by holding himself available to answer questions as they arose during the course of my study.

1

FROM CABIN
TO CONGRESS

LATE IN THE AFTERNOON of a chilly autumn day Electra Eliza Barkley and her husband John wound their way down the quarter-mile path that led from their farm to the log cabin owned by John's father, Alben. Eliza's pleasant, but slight, angular face was marred by an occasional wince as she clutched the broad hand of her husband. John, with his ruddy complexion, bushy mustache, and characteristically large Barkley ears, embodied the soil as the true descendant of a long line of farmers. The number of blankets and extra supplies he carried indicated this would not be a typical social visit to his family's homestead.

The visit, though unusual, was not unplanned. When Eliza had realized she was pregnant with her first child, she turned to her mother-in-law, Amanda, the best midwife in Wheel, Kentucky, a small community nestled between the villages of Lowes and Fancy Farm on the northwestern edge of Graves County. On the morning of November 24, 1877, at 3:30 A.M., Willie Alben Barkley was born. Despite the later jests of wags, Barkley did not greet life with his famous rendition of "Wagon Wheels." Instead, he shattered the peaceful early morning with a screech—quite normal for a newborn babe.

Alben's humble birth in a log cabin might not have been

the gateway through which he moved into a world of politics had it not been for his parents' habit of calling him by his middle name. As the given name for an aspiring American politician, Willie left something to be desired. When Alben attained an age old enough to assert his own views on the matter, he changed his name from Willie Alben to Alben William and laid a scourge upon anyone who dared to call him Willie.

Although John Barkley seldom began his day before 6:00 A.M., the reality of nineteenth-century country life belies the romantic notions of twentieth-century urban dwellers. Added to the burdens of an extraordinarily rugged existence was the fact that he was a tenant tobacco farmer. The poor reddish-brown topsoil covering the undulating terrain of the fifty-acre farm demanded greater efforts for bountiful yields in this generally impoverished area of western Kentucky.

When John completed his own chores, he sold his labor to wealthier neighbors for a dollar a day. Only later in life would he briefly achieve a lifelong dream to work his own farm. John's absence and the scarcity of money forced Eliza to fill her hours by maintaining the home and making every conceivable household and personal item from clothes to soaps. From time to time she had to entrust Alben to the care of his grandmother.

Amanda was an outspoken person in an era and area known for its hardworking but silent women. His grandmother introduced young Alben to politics. She brightened his childhood with stories of her own youth, when her playmates included Adlai Stevenson, later vice president under Grover Cleveland, and James McKenzie, a congressman from Kentucky. Stevenson's grandson, also named Adlai, would compete successfully against cousin Alben for the 1952 Democratic presidential nomination.

With such remarkable and prominent relatives, Alben probably did not realize that he was poor until a family shopping trip to Mayfield when he was twelve revealed that store clerks wore Sunday suits during the week. He had, though, little time to contemplate his humble surroundings. From an early age he had to accept his share of work. As the Barkley family grew larger (it eventually increased to eight children) and Alben grew older, he began to assist his father on the farm, to help his mother with household chores, and to watch over his younger brothers and sisters. The interludes between sessions in country schools were filled with chopping wood, splitting rails, digging out stumps, setting tobacco, plowing fields, and dozens of other back-breaking tasks. By the age of fourteen, the slender but sturdy Alben toiled in fields as a hired hand and lightened the day by swapping tales with fellow workers, many of whom were blacks.

Alben escaped some of the prejudices of his age despite the fact that the people of Graves County had possessed strong sympathies for the South during the Civil War. A primeval equality emerged from the hard rural life, reinforced in part by the old English custom of calling out each year all males regardless of race and fortune to improve county roads. These positive values were strengthened in Alben by a happy but strict upbringing by religious parents. John held the position of elder in the Presbyterian church of Lowes, and Eliza refused to light the stove on Sundays unless the pastor joined them for dinner. Liquor and playing cards never entered the home so, without prepackaged electronic entertainments, Alben learned the art of conversation.

In spite of example and admonition, the boy shared escapades which agitated his parents. The rough-and-tumble world of rural Kentucky impressed on Alben the need for courage. Amiably inclined, the boy nonetheless had many physical encounters. The tensions of workaday life found relief only in crude forms of play, an occasional fair, and weekly visits to church and one of Lowes's two general stores. Joys were simple and fleeting: a glass of lemonade, a mouthful of sugar, a trip to Mayfield or Clinton. All too soon, in his parents' opinion, Alben discovered smoking tobacco and pretty girls.

3

Alben barely reached adolescence when his interest in girls led him to make his first speech. The Presbyterian church sponsored Children's Day each year, and youngsters prepared speeches to edify their elders. Alben would not have been on the program had he not been bewitched by Sadie Ward, the pastor's daughter, and volunteered his services to impress her. He went over the piece he had been given to memorize so many times he thought he could recite it forwards and backwards, but shortly before his big day arrived one of the church elders, a mischievous fellow named Joseph Dunn, kidded Alben by telling him that he would forget the whole thing when he stood up before the audience.

Alben laughed, but when Children's Day came and his name was called he stood at the rostrum and saw only the twinkling eyes of Joseph Dunn. "From that moment," Barkley later recalled, "my memorized and practiced recitation departed completely and it never returned then or thereafter." Humbled and shamed, Alben returned to his pew. He learned that speechmaking required a different sort of courage than roughhousing with the boys. His budding and one-sided romance with the pastor's daughter suffered an early and severe frost, but his love for oratory had just begun.

In 1892 John Barkley made a decision of great importance to Alben's future. With the help of friends and neighbors, the family packed three wagons, tied their Jersey cow to one, and moved twenty-five miles southwest from Lowes to Clinton, the Hickman County seat. The nearby Mississippi River and the town's two colleges combined to provide Alben with a cultural atmosphere far in excess of anything he had experienced in Lowes. The move little helped the family fortunes, for John, expert in tobacco, found meager success in raising corn. Despite John's failure to improve the family's status through farming, Alben was able to fulfill his youthful desire for a college education. Shortly after the family had settled into the new home, Alben enrolled in Marvin College.

Alben never graduated from a high school, but then to describe Marvin as a "college" in modern terms would be as impossible as equating Alben's country education with the rigid K-12 grades so familiar to us today. Marvin, a Methodist school no longer in existence, accepted adolescents and trained them for adulthood. A single building housed most of its activities, and Alben could remember years later the names and count the numbers of his class of 1897 on a single hand. In this intimate and personal atmosphere, Alben's fine mind, which had been stimulated mainly by the raw frontierlike life of Lowes, grew with the knowledge and civilizing influences of tradition and the humanities. He would also become a lifelong Methodist.

Alben attended college only because one of Marvin's two presidents, J. C. Speight, had the compassion and flexibility necessary to enable young Barkley to take advantage of his proximity to the school. Speight allowed Alben to miss the first and last months of each academic year in order to assist his father with the family farm. More importantly, Speight granted the young man a janitorial scholarship which met all his academic expenses. These benign actions on the part of Marvin's young president occurred out of recognition for Alben's determination and promise. The farm boy later repaid his benefactor by appointing Speight's son, Edmund, to the United States Naval Academy at Annapolis as one of his first acts as congressman.

Thus Alben's pursuit of classics and a Bachelor of Arts degree combined with the daily drudgery of sweeping rooms, making fires, carrying water, and dusting furniture. When the teenager grew older and gained fame, a plaque placed on the building announced appropriately, "BARKLEY SWEPT HERE." Janitorial duties and hard work on the farm had not prevented his enjoying the intellectual and social excitement that accompanies college life. No stigma was attached to his duties. His peers could not boast a much higher social station and they admired Alben's perseverance. The close-knit students participated equally both in the trials and tribulations of learning and in the lighter moments of school—hay rides, square dances, and swimming parties to Columbus, Kentucky, by the Mississippi River. The exuberant youngster also shared dates with most of Marvin's few coeds.

The afflictions of various cases of teenage infatuations did not detract Alben from his one constant love, speechmaking. He joined Marvin's Periclean Debating Society and added a touch of country tenaciousness, if not brilliance, to the society's contests as he thundered home his points against opponents. The flora and fauna surrounding Clinton learned tolerance as he practiced his speeches hour by hour. He took literally to stumping the woods around his father's farm, and his oral practice produced results.

The self-confidence he gained through practice and the presence of mind he developed through contests marked a sharp contrast with his dismal performance on Children's Day in Lowes. During an oratorical contest at Marvin, Alben's forceful gesture unhinged one of his snap-on shirt cuffs and, consequently, disturbed his train of thought. Instead of meekly heading for a nearby exit, he captured the judges' attentions by sweeping his arm through the air and adjusting with a dramatic flair the distended and loosened cuff. At the same time he forced his mind back to the speech he had memorized and regained his composure. He finished the speech so brilliantly that the judges, amazed by his nonchalant handling of a distracting incident, awarded him the gold medal.

When Barkley completed his studies at Marvin, he wanted only two things from life: to become a lawyer and to enter politics. The consistency of his aspirations is quite evident. As a youngster he had been regaled by his family, and in particular by his grandmother, with stories about his political relatives. Politics and elections provided an integral part of the entertainments enjoyed by the strongly Democratic area around Lowes. Alben's country teachers, Gertrude Backus and Elizabeth Lowe, encouraged his dreams and expressed, if not seriously at least with great kindness, the hope he might someday become president of the United States. At Marvin, Barkley's concern for oratory and political issues reflected only too well the direction of his desires for the future. His mentor and patron, President Speight, kindled Alben's bent for politics by running successfully for the Kentucky State Senate in 1896.

By graduation time Alben had decided to attend Emory College, then at Oxford, Georgia, to pursue the study of law. A perennial problem, money, raised an ugly impediment before his ambition. Out of desperation, Barkley accepted a summer job in 1897 selling cooking crockery farm to farm on horseback in his "territory," the southern portion of Graves County. Slender, dressed in his best suit, with his rich brown wavy hair slicked back, and carrying samples in a satchel, the dapper young man on his rented black horse looked every inch the prosperous doctor. Only the slight exaggeration and prominence of his nose, ears, and full mouth prevented him from being viewed as downright handsome.

"Doc" Barkley used his good looks and his experience at speech to press home his sales. A single problem interfered with his success. His company's crockery cracked when put to the flame. The strict, religious upbringing Alben experienced as a child led him to return to each farm and to pay out of his own pocket for all losses incurred by the farmwives. Dejected and discouraged, Barkley found all his efforts were for naught, but at the last moment he was able to borrow two hundred dollars to cover his tuition and expenses for school.

Barkley spent one academic year at Emory, but the problems of money continued to plague him and forced his return to Clinton. Determined to pay his debts and to earn enough to resume his studies, he accepted eagerly an appointment as instructor at Marvin College. The position he acquired, however, paid only twenty-five dollars a month. Taking the job turned out to be one of the worst decisions Barkley ever made. The liveliness of his classroom was not due solely to his intellectual abilities. Too many of his students had also known their instructor as a student whose nickname, "Monk," had more to do with monkeyshines

7

than scholarship. How was Barkley to keep discipline when he had shared pranks with half his charges and dates with the other half? His interest in reading law grew in direct proportion to his perception of an endless school term.

As the academic year moved interminably toward the Christmas recess, Barkley discovered a compelling reason to sever his professional relations with Marvin and resume his studies of jurisprudence. His father had forsaken finally the unrewarding task of trying to eke out a living on the farm. The family went to Paducah where John Barkley took employment in a cotton cordage mill. The elder Barkley exchanged his skill as a farmer for the security of a paycheck.

The fateful move played directly into Alben's hand. Realizing his uncertain abilities as a teacher and begging the need to follow his family, Barkley resigned from Marvin in midterm to join his parents in Paducah. This minor change in geography marked a major change in his life. In Paducah, Barkley committed himself to the law and walked with the sure tread of a man with a goal. He would mature professionally in McCracken County and his name would become synonymous with the city of Paducah.

Just twenty-one on his arrival at the end of 1898, Barkley's assets consisted of a few shirts, fifty cents change, and a letter of introduction to Charles K. Wheeler, lawyer and congressman. Wheeler engaged the young man to clerk in his office and permitted him to study law during his free moments. The shrewd politician's generosity was more apparent than real and reflected poorly his position as an inflationary free-silver Democrat. His new clerk's salary added up to zero as Wheeler balanced Barkley's inexperience at clerking with his benefit from reading Wheeler's books.

Besides studying and clerking during the day, Barkley learned shorthand at night in order to earn a few dollars taking depositions. To keep body and soul together, he relied on Saturday jobs to bring him immediate cash. At one shoe store where he clerked, a big man with even bigger feet entered and stated, "I'd like to see a pair of shoes that would

8

fit me." Barkley shot back, "So would I!" Overwork exaggerated his sense of humor and for many of his employers, Barkley's part-time jobs became onetime affairs.

After several months, it dawned on Barkley that he could ill afford financially, physically, and mentally the congressman's concept of generosity. Fortunately, Wheeler's rival, the gold Democrat John K. Hendrick, and his law partner, Judge William S. Bishop, took pity on the young clerk and hired him at twelve dollars a month to do what he had been doing for nothing for Wheeler. Although Hendrick's move did not redeem his loss to Wheeler in the 1896 congressional race, his small act of spite turned out to be a whopping victory for Barkley.

Saved from poverty, Barkley received more than physical nourishment from his work and pay. Hendrick and Bishop boasted one of the finer law libraries on Paducah's "legal row," and in Bishop, Barkley gained proximity to one of the better legal minds in western Kentucky. Good luck, hard work, and foresight paid additional dividends to the determined young man. His study of stenography allowed him later to seek and accept a job as court reporter for the McCracken County District Court.

The happier and more profitable surroundings enabled Barkley to pass his bar examination, pay off his debts, and set up his own office—all within the space of three years. Even after he began the practice of law he continued to perform the duties of court reporter to supplement his income. He would later jest that his position with the county court, not his small practice, kept him afloat financially.

The reality of steady cases belies his humble boast. In the early years of the twentieth century, Paducah was a colorful and not quite tame Ohio River town full of energy, pride, and conflicts. This provided the new lawyer with ample work. In the summer of 1902, Barkley could actually afford the luxury of taking special law courses at the University of Virginia. By the following year, he had saved over eight hundred dollars, enough money, he felt, to be able to marry.

9

In Paducah, Barkley had met Dorothy Brower, a store-keeper's daughter. Five years younger than he, Dorothy looked frail, but possessed a dark sophisticated appearance and a slightly whimsical smile that piqued his interest. Barkley seems not to have fathomed the depth of his love until she accompanied her family when they left Paducah for Tiptonville, Tennessee. The newest of Paducah's lawyers spent long hours writing or traveling to see Dorothy and when in 1903 he had saved enough money he proposed to, was accepted by, and married the young woman in June of that year. Most of the eight hundred dollars went as a down payment for a gas-lit, four-room, white frame cottage.

Having spent most of his years in a nomadic existence moving from one rented house to another, he felt immediately that his life was twice blessed. Actually, the product of their love brought additional blessings: their children David (1906), Marian (1909), and Laura Louise (1911). Over the next six years the burgeoning family forced the Barkleys to move twice. Their second move was to a two-story frame on Jefferson Street in Paducah, which remained their permanent Kentucky residence until 1937.

In the first years of marriage, Barkley continued his practice of law and his reporting for the district court. He also joined the Woodmen of the World, Elks, Odd Fellows, Zenda Club, and Improved Order of Red Men. In fact, very few reputable organizations in Paducah did not list him on their rolls as a member and officer. He maintained his aim to enter politics, and his membership in every conceivable civic and social group certainly mirrored his ambitions for the future and provided him a platform for speeches and contacts.

However, people meant much to Barkley, not in the abstract, but in the flesh—he simply enjoyed talking and being with others. And his friends and neighbors responded positively to his outgoing personality, to the warmth of his interest in their well-being. Almost inevitably he jumped into politics by running for county attorney in 1905. It would be hard to locate a lower rung on the political ladder, but this apprenticeship served him well.

Success came to Barkley precisely because he conducted himself in that campaign with the same tireless effort and drive that characterized his youth. He proclaimed his candidacy in December 1904 and then borrowed a mule, swapped it for a one-eyed horse named Dick, and proceeded to stump the county on horseback. At first the odds were stacked heavily against him. He challenged the Democratic courthouse clique by running against the incumbent, Eugene A. Graves, who was looking forward to a third term. The principal issues would thus be Barkley's youth and Graves's experience. On foot or on horseback, Barkley canvassed the county and argued that as county court reporter he had experience aplenty and that Graves's grasping designs to retain office were simply undemocratic.

The twenty-seven-year-old aspirant slept where he stopped. He certainly delivered many speeches, though much of his support came from farmers who promised their votes after Barkley assisted them in their chores. The son of a farmer became the farmers' politician. When the date for the primary arrived at the end of March 1905, Barkley lost to Graves in Paducah, but county farmers gave him their votes and his victory. He then ran unopposed in the general election and in January 1906 he took office. For the next four years he built a strong reputation for honesty and diligence. He prosecuted well the several hundred criminal cases that came within his purview, including the cases of two crooked fiscal court magistrates, and he upheld keenly the citizens' interests in advising the county government.

As it turned out, Barkley's honesty as a county attorney paid off handsomely when he decided to run in the 1909 elections for county judge. That particular campaign degenerated into one of the ugliest, scandal-ridden affairs he would face in his political career. Even if he had foreseen the character of his upcoming struggle when the *Paducah News-Democrat* announced his candidacy on August 22,

1908, he surely would still have run for the office. The county judgeship was the next logical step he had to take if he ever hoped to achieve state or national prominence.

Less than three months later Barkley's friend and county clerk since 1897, Hiram Smedley, was indicted for keeping property tax payments from the fiscal court. The eight elected magistrates of that body appointed Barkley to head a special three-man committee to check the books for several specific instances of fraud. The report indicated that Smedley's pilfering had cost the county $1,582.50. Unfortunately, this was only the beginning of the scandal.

The hyperactive, greedy, and amateurish Smedley suffered arrest for twenty counts of forgery in May. To add a further touch of seaminess to this scenario, Smedley's drug addiction prompted a lunacy hearing for toxic insanity. And the worst was yet to come. In August as the political campaign shifted into high gear, a complete audit of the county books showed a loss of $16,000, of which only $6,000 could be traced directly to Smedley. In Democratic-controlled McCracken County it seemed that what Smedley failed to acquire went into Democratic coffers. After several trials, a spell in the Hopkinsville asylum, and six years in the Kentucky penitentiary, Smedley managed to keep his silence about coconspirators. At least one scholar, Gerald S. Grinde, has implied that Barkley may have known something about these sordid affairs but actual proof is missing, since the 1937 Ohio River flood destroyed county records.

Regardless, these disclosures dampened Barkley's campaign and put him, uncharacteristically, on the defensive. Whether he was involved in the Smedley affair meant less in the campaign than the fact he had been elected in 1905 on the same ticket as the apparently corrupt courthouse gang. Republican opponent Thomas N. Hazelip urged voters, naturally enough, to clean out all Democratic county officials, guilty or not of embezzling funds. The Republican took the offensive in September 1909 and challenged Barkley to a series of debates. The county attorney could ill afford the luxury of turning him down. Ominously enough, the debates opened on the same date as Smedley's lunacy trial.

Barkley left little to chance. He honed his oratorical skills in debate to a fine edge and, for added insurance, brought county clerk candidate Gus Singleton and a bevy of male cheerleaders along to aid his cause with heckles or applause as the occasion required. Defensively he argued that Hazelip's charge of guilt by association was reprehensible and "enough to disgust decent people." Then, and in later debates, Barkley pushed forward his record that revealed his eminent qualifications for the county judgeship.

Hazelip could not fault Barkley's efficient and progressive nature. Even Republicans had to admit that he had saved the taxpayers over $35,000 by his stern challenge to fraudulent claims against the county. And no one could question his honest devotion to the people's interest. Barkley garnered 54.5 percent of the vote, less than expected, but more than achieved by most other Democrats in what proved to be a Republican year in a Democratic county. Republicans would dominate the fiscal court, for example, by a margin of five to three.

After Barkley took the oath of office in January 1910, he learned firsthand that the duties of county judge had less to do with courtroom procedures than the title implied. The judge was head of county affairs and performed a wide range of duties and functions. In his very first act he officiated at a wedding. It was one job he forgot he would have and he bungled it badly, although the couple seemed impervious to his nervous recitation. After this shaky start, Barkley's administration moved smoothly enough in predictable directions. The recent scandals prompted him to recommend the frequent audit of county records and the close scrutiny of claims by the fiscal court. But the focus of his attentions fell on the improvement of county roads.

He pledged to gravel main roads, and, although generally conservative in fiscal affairs, Barkley burdened with debt the road and bridge fund to accomplish his purpose. In addition, these improvements were made through private contracts that allowed farmers seasonal employment and pay

13

for work that had been done for free in years gone by. There is little doubt that Barkley paid off a debt to the memory of his and his father's hard labor and to the farmers who had supported his campaign.

The final fortuitous circumstance in the first half of Barkley's life was the fact that Ollie James, a powerhouse orator and, after 1900, perennial First District congressman, decided to vacate his district to seek a seat in the United States Senate in 1912. In his established pattern, Barkley announced in December 1911 his candidacy early and waited patiently for the opposition to form. Since his party tightly controlled First District counties in western Kentucky, the Democratic primary would decide the election.

By February 1912 a Mayfield politician, Joseph E. Robbins, tossed his hat into the ring, but then developed second thoughts. He told the McCracken County judge that he would withdraw at Barkley's pleasure. Since both men possessed strong attributes, the likelihood that additional candidates would compete against the pair appeared remote. Barkley's ambition led him to make a costly error. Instead of waiting for the primary's approach, he asked Robbins to announce his intentions immediately. Within a month after the compliance on March 23, Barkley discovered he would face not an opponent of straw but three serious contenders: Commonwealth Attorney Denny Smith from Trigg County, Ballard County Judge Jacob Corbett, and John Hendrick, Barkley's old mentor and benefactor.

During the summer of 1912, the four candidates joined together in canvassing the district and sharing the expenses. The only real issues in the campaign involved Barkley's relative youth and supposedly radical views. His call for federal aid to road construction smacked of socialism to his opponents.

As the summer wore on and the Democratic National Convention selected Woodrow Wilson as its candidate and adopted a progressive party platform, Barkley's positions moved in perfect alignment with the progressive wing of party and country. The McCracken County judge turned

the arguments against him into assets. His relative youth became needed energy and his radical views became party
loyalty. When the election was held, a steady drizzle drove
farmers from the fields to the newly surfaced roads and into
the polling stations. By the end of August 3, Barkley
amassed nearly half the votes cast and entered a new phase
in his life.

It would be easy to claim that Barkley's progressive image
formed gradually over a period of years and culminated in
the 1912 election campaign. In actual fact, the origins of his
physical stamina and good-natured humor would be sim-
pler to reconstruct than the more complex patterns of his
ideas. The eminent faith he held in the individual was tempered by his experience as a tenant farmer's son who realized that rural and urban dwellers alike required services
and regulations that only society at large could provide. His
desire for lower tariffs, railroad regulation, and government
assistance with road building fitted neatly into the agrarian
mold cast by Populist and Democrat William Jennings
Bryan. But Barkley espoused these issues instinctively, not
ideologically. He admitted later that during his college and
early lawyer days he opposed the several bids Bryan made
for the presidency before 1908, and he belonged for years to
the conservative gold wing of the Democratic party. Despite
his later support for expensive governmental programs and
despite the generally chaotic and deficit nature of his personal finances, Barkley retained a strong streak of fiscal restraint.

In 1908 Barkley's reputation as an excellent speaker and
party regular gained reward through his appointment to the
Democratic Speakers' Bureau. Thus partisan politics and
the flattery of statewide recognition led him to campaign
for the Bryan ticket. The position also allowed him to build
friendships and political debts in those western Kentucky
counties that comprise the First Congressional District. By
1912 he appeared to be an amalgam of reform-minded leaders Bryan, Theodore Roosevelt, and Woodrow Wilson. But
the position he took in favor of prohibition grew directly out

of his strict upbringing and dislike for liquor. Other progressive issues, whether child labor laws or the federal income tax, he seemed to adopt for pragmatic reasons that satisfied his ambitions as much as his convictions. When he accepted the party's platform in 1912, Barkley went to the offensive and offered the electorate a clear choice. His tactics coupled with his strong rural support proved overwhelming for his generally more conservative opponents. Fate, in the circumstances of his birth, education, and early political career, played a disproportionate role in governing his first thirty-five years. For the next fourteen years it would be the United States House of Representatives and the influence of President Wilson that would promote, refine, and strengthen Barkley's political and sometimes liberal social views.

2

THE PROGRESSIVE

ALBEN W. BARKLEY's entrance into Washington, D.C., in March 1913 paralleled remarkably his arrival into Paducah fourteen years earlier. The recently elected congressman possessed little besides his certificate of election to the House of Representatives. His costly primary campaign, a needlessly incurred expense, left him bereft of funds. The tightrope he walked between financial deprivation and despair forced the Barkleys to decide that Alben would have to live in Washington alone. The nation's capital was an overgrown southern town in 1913, and among the few entertainments available to its residents were the political conflicts on Capitol Hill. Thus Barkley could live frugally at the Congress Hotel on his substantial but unfrivolous annual salary of $7,500 and slowly replenish his funds. The reputation and experience he had amassed in McCracken County counted for even less in Washington than had his obscure status when he entered Paducah. He would be only one of 114 new Democratic congressmen, formerly state and local officials of every description, and he would have to prove himself all over again.

Barkley's new role, however, allowed him to identify strongly with President Woodrow Wilson. Inexperience and an uncertain reputation characterized the new president's administration as much as they did Barkley's initiation to the Congress. A Virginia-born son of a Presbyterian minister, Wilson had an elongated face, pince-nez, high fore-head, and graying hair, all of which stereotyped him accurately as a college professor. He had received a Ph.D. from Johns Hopkins, taught political economy at Princeton University, and eventually had become that institution's presiding officer. In 1910 Wilson put his training to practice as governor of New Jersey. Although he mirrored the progressive mood of the country, Wilson two years later surprised the Democratic National Convention by becoming its nominee and then surprised the nation by becoming its president. At the convention, Wilson's dark-horse candidacy won the race against three formidable contenders. Victory came to him nationally because the opposition split between the Bull Moose Theodore Roosevelt and the regular Republican William Howard Taft.

Wilson's New Freedom program sought to resurrect competition in the American economy and to emancipate the individual and small businessman from what appeared to the president to be the crushing designs of Wall Street monopoly. Although inflexibility and aloofness fatally marred Wilson's character, he reserved for friends a winning smile and a charming personality. Furthermore he had a penchant for cultivating the favor of those lawmakers who were joining him for the first time in Washington. Many of these men, including Barkley, would revere Wilson with almost religious fervor.

On March 4, 1913, Wilson and Barkley recited their oaths of office, but the two men would not have an opportunity for an extended meeting until April 22, when Barkley had his first interview with the new president. Wilson immediately gained the Kentucky First District congressman's complete allegiance for several excellent reasons. First, their characters shared certain abiding similarities: an adamant belief in party, a strong sense of regional heritage, and a moral flair derived from a richly endowed religious upbringing. Incidentally the two men were absolutely delighted to discover that they both had learned and used stenographic skills—Barkley as a law clerk and Wilson as a college professor.

Second, the pair evinced a partisan attitude so shrill as to make of the word *independent* an unconscionably foul term. But Wilson exercised a far more sophisticated and developed ideology than Barkley. The president admired the British system wherein a prime minister ruled because he led the majority party and the government, in turn, survived because it unified that party to approve important measures in Parliament. In the Democratic-controlled Sixty-third Congress, Wilson achieved remarkable success, since, much like an English prime minister, he mustered the votes necessary to approve legislation. House Majority Leader Oscar W. Underwood, for example, employed the binding party caucus to assure passage of those bills the administration considered vital. Ostensibly, at least, the integration of purpose between president and Congress was formidable. Barkley, who had grown up in a one-party region, had viewed office as a natural reward for partisanship. Wilson, however, would show the congressman that the end of party activity was not a mere office but rather a philosophy and an ability to implement programs. Hence, for these men, party and partisanship formed the very foundation of America's democratic institutions.

Third, lofty principles aside, a financial aspect also cemented the political relationship between Wilson and Barkley. Understandably, the president wanted the congressman's vote and support for administration-sponsored measures in the House of Representatives. Proportionately, however, Wilson was far more important to Barkley and the other new congressmen. The legislators' reelection in the next campaign would hinge on their ability to produce for their constituents a record of success, tying them inevitably to the fortunes of the Wilson administration. Also, the congressmen's main source of payment or patronage for their political debts lay in their presidentially sanctioned power to appoint postmasters in their districts. Thus Barkley's first interview with the president on April 22, as well as those immediately subsequent, focused on patronage.

The patronage issue had been complicated by the sometimes politically adroit Republican President Taft. He had played a clever trick on the Democrats by a blanket draft without benefit of examination of all fourth-class or rural postmasters into the civil service. Since most of the appointees were Republicans, this action was especially irritating in Democratic strongholds such as Barkley's district. Barkley secured Wilson's promise at least to implement competitive examinations for that category of postmaster. Later, the president assisted Barkley with another postal problem. When a higher category vacancy occurred in Mayfield and no fewer than ten strident Barkley supporters filed applications to become that city's postmaster, Wilson rescued Barkley from this dilemma by assuming the congressman's prerogative and selecting a relative of one of his own Princeton University colleagues. Barkley could not have been more pleased by Wilson's actions. After he requested and received Wilson's letter explaining his choice, the congressman promptly publicized the letter in Mayfield, thereby sparing himself the ire of nine disappointed office-seekers. Not only did Barkley avoid making a no-win decision, but also Wilson's well-reasoned letter of explanation turned a stumbling block into a stepping-stone as Barkley retained the political sympathy of his Mayfield friends.

Shortly after his first meeting with the president, Barkley delivered his maiden speech before the House of Representatives on April 24. Wilson had specified in his Inaugural Address several reforms designed to redeem the pledges he and the party had made to the electorate during the fall campaign. The first of these major pieces of legislation introduced and ultimately passed in September 1913 became known as the Underwood-Simmons Tariff. Through this reform the Democrats fulfilled their promise to reverse the trend and attitude of protectionism for American industry that the Republicans had strengthened through high taxes or tariffs on foreign imports. When House-sponsor Underwood honored Barkley by designating the freshman congressman to speak on behalf of the lower tariff bill, Barkley required neither prodding nor prompting to argue forcefully for the measure. From firsthand experience Barkley knew that those of his constituents raising dark tobacco sold it abroad on ruthlessly competitive foreign markets, yet the protective tariff forced them to purchase various American products and supplies at artificially high prices. The tariff had been the focus of farmers' frustration for decades and was fundamental in prompting the Populist movement's organization of rural dissatisfaction.

Although Barkley demonstrated little originality in his arguments for the lower tariff, his presentation evidenced certain characteristics that remained with him for the rest of his life: he worked hard to master the complex problems involved in legislation; he sided with progressive Democrats; and, while he chastised Republican opponents, he did so with a digestible humor that made his enemies few and his jokes famous. In the tariff speech Barkley particularly drew Democratic applause for his litany of Republican sins. "When the people have asked for free lumber in order that they might build humble homes in which to abide," Barkley proceeded sarcastically, "the Republicans have responded by placing acorns upon the free list. . . . When we have asked for cheaper milk, they have responded with free dragon's blood." The congressman further won the laughter of his colleagues and the attention of the press by concluding his speech with the anecdote of a Kentucky farmer who searched for a better life by moving west to Colorado and then Kansas. Republican policies and natural disasters, however, forced the hapless farmer and his family back home. As he reentered Kentucky, the farmer wrote on his wagon:

Colorado irrigation,
Kansas winds and conflagration,
High tariff and taxation,
Bill Taft's administration,

Roosevelt's vociferation,
Hell-fire and damnation,
Bring me back to my wife's relations.

Barkley's partisan attitude would later cause critics to describe him erroneously as a slavish me-too follower of Democratic leadership. Yet even in these early years of national service, Barkley revealed an independent streak that belied an image of the unthinking drone. He spoke at times for amendments the administration considered undesirable. Against the direct wishes of President Wilson, the Kentucky congressman also upheld a campaign pledge by introducing a bill to eliminate those unproductive lame-duck sessions that allowed defeated members of the House and Senate to serve from January to March after an election year. Although the president expressed sympathy with Barkley's position, he refused to support him out of deference to other priority items pending in Congress. Barkley's colleagues agreed with the president and failed to approve the bill. The "lame duck" legislation would have to await another decade, sponsor, and president before being passed into law.

Nonetheless, and not unexpectedly, most of Barkley's endeavors were consistent with his role as an advocate for Wilson's programs. For example, in his Inaugural Address, the president had called for currency-banking reforms and measures to restrict monopoly and reinstate competition in American business. Congress responded, albeit in altered form, with the Federal Reserve Act (1913), Clayton Anti-Trust Act (1914), and the Federal Trade Commission Act (1914). Barkley's generally enthusiastic support for these reforms and his gregarious personality made him open to warm relationships with such party leaders as House Speaker Champ Clark and other noted congressmen.

Recompense for his oratorical skills and humorous defense of Democratic bills occurred early in his new career when Barkley became the first freshman congressman to preside over the House of Representatives. In his memoirs, *That Reminds Me*, Barkley said that it took every ounce of self-control that he possessed not to declare at least in jest the entire Republican party out of order. He would later punish his associates when he closed a session of Congress with his warbling rendition of "My Old Kentucky Home." More significant than these honors and lighter activities, perhaps, was Barkley's appointment to the prestigious and exclusive Interstate and Foreign Commerce Committee— exclusive because members of that overworked group could hold no other committee assignment in Congress. While he may have wished to join the Rivers and Harbors Committee for the possible benefits his district might derive in funds and patronage, the Interstate and Foreign Commerce Committee offered him important work and immediate responsibility that he otherwise would have missed.

Barkley returned to Paducah and his district in October 1913 to visit his family and to make a few quick campaign speeches on behalf of several Democratic candidates during the fall elections. Former President Taft's decision to place fourth-class postmasters under the umbrella protection of the civil service severely curtailed Barkley's ability to dispense patronage. Instead he had to repay his political debts through favorable speeches for candidates whose abilities and characters were sometimes questionable. However, the biggest debt Barkley owed himself. Life in Washington during his first congressional term proved hectic but not hectic enough to vanquish the crushing loneliness he felt without Dorothy and the children. The hardest blow awaited Barkley when the family was reunited—two-year-old Laura Louise did not recognize her father. Heedless of expense or inconvenience, Barkley decided his family must accompany him for the next session of Congress.

Upon Barkley's return to Washington, he found lodgings that permitted the family to join him early in 1914. Over the next several years they resided in a number of rented apartments. The ease with which Barkley won reelection in 1914 and thereafter (at times he ran unopposed in the primary) allowed the family the luxury of considering his work in Washington permanent. So in the early 1920s they pur-

23

chased a three-story home on Cleveland Avenue, and by then the family could even afford a cook and a yardman to help with domestic chores. Regardless of changing circumstances, the Barkleys remained a loyal and close-knit group. David Barkley later remembered fondly that they always ate dinner together, and in the evenings the congressman led them in playing spelling games or amused them with political stories. There were trials and tribulations, but the home was "filled," as Laura recalled, "with laughter and good humor." During frequent breaks in Congress the Barkleys would take automobile tours to historic shrines or would return to their house in Paducah. The nation's capital, however, eventually became the real home for David, Marian, and Laura, and their father had to remind them to tell Kentucky visitors and press representatives that they were from Paducah. The politician even went so far as to dock his children's allowance every time they forgot the name of a constituent.

While the Barkley family's move to Washington in 1914 proved a momentous and fortuitous change in the congressman's existence, events in Europe cast a dark shadow over the United States which eventually touched the lives of every American family. The assassination in June of the heir to the throne of the Austro-Hungarian Empire led to the mobilization of armies and the implementation of agreements in the alliance systems that pitted the Entente Powers of England, France, and Russia against the Central Powers of Germany, Austria-Hungary, and Italy. The latter switched sides in 1915, but the strength of the Central Powers was augmented, at least on paper, by the Ottoman Empire. Expansionist dreams coupled with commercial, military, and national rivalries formed the backdrop for the start of one of the most gruesome and bloody conflicts on the sordid side of man's history, a conflict which contemporaries dubbed euphemistically "The Great War." Only later would a second and more ghastly struggle permit man to number his follies and describe this earlier devastating period as World War I.

Even though President Wilson asked Americans to be neutral in word and deed, Europe's civil war intruded increasingly on the domestic affairs of the United States. The first, most obvious area struck by European events was America's foreign commerce, evidenced in the war's chilling effect on international trade. The preponderance of English seapower swept the Central Powers' shipping from the oceans, and the Entente countries pressed their merchant marines into war service. By 1914 the United States had become almost totally dependent on foreign shipping; its transoceanic fleet numbered fifteen vessels of which nine were passenger ships. Reduced shipping services and exorbitant fees charged by those ships willing and available to cross submarine-infested seas threatened to clamp an unwanted embargo on American goods produced for foreign markets. As early as the summer of 1914 the president called for the purchase of an American-owned merchant fleet, but the proposal aroused the strident opposition of most Republicans and many Democrats. The potential destruction of United States ships at sea could lead to America's declaration of war against the offending belligerent. A greater concern to conservative lawmakers, though, was that the government's purchase and operation of ships would be socialism, pure and simple.

Congressman Barkley disagreed vocally with that conservative point of view. When the bill was reintroduced before the 1915 lame-duck session of Congress, Barkley assumed considerable leadership in the argument for its passage. The reason is easy to discern. Five-sixths of Kentucky's First District dark tobacco went into foreign markets. Although the congressman himself had given up tobacco smoking, his pragmatic logic illuminated for him the need to sell American products, including tobacco, on foreign markets. Much as people's needs had led him to "socialistic" opinions on government-improved roads, this situation prompted Barkley's disregard for "worn-out political aphorisms" which dictated that less government is better government. He perceived a problem which only the country as a whole could solve. "Shall we sit," Barkley asked rhetorically, "with folded hands and complacent consciences and say this great Government has no remedy to offer her people?" His peers in the House agreed overwhelmingly with his position, but a Senate filibuster caused the bill to suffer an agonizing death. Furthermore, the failure of the Senate to concur with Barkley and the House slowly undermined Wilson's call for neutrality. While the Entente controlled the surface of the ocean, the Central Powers operated underneath. The very nature of the situation meant that America's foreign commerce depended on neutral or Entente shipping and when destroyed it would be by German submarines.

In May 1915 a German U-boat sank the Cunard line passenger ship *Lusitania*. The catastrophic loss of 1,200 lives, including 128 United States nationals, illustrates the second way Europe's war intruded on American interests. Between the destruction German submarines unleashed and the restriction English surface vessels imposed on neutral shipping, the United States seemed to lose control of her destiny and her ability to protect American life and property, particularly on the high seas. Later, the Wilson administration demanded and gained Germany's pledge to restrict underwater warfare; in 1915, however, many in Congress devoted their energies to improving America's military strength. Barkley remained lukewarm toward the issue of preparedness, and his silence on the army appropriation bill speaks enough for his views. Even so, he was not a pacifist. Physically and mentally, pound for pound, the rugged farmer's son possessed as much strength and courage as any contemporary in or out of Congress. Nor was he mindlessly oblivious to foreign affairs. The arguments he used for the ship purchase bill and the numerous speeches he made for his constituents reveal that he read widely and tried desperately to understand and interpret the world's problems. Nevertheless, he felt more comfortable in domestic rather than in foreign affairs.

Not only did Barkley respond unenthusiastically to improving the army, but he voted blatantly against naval appropriations. A simple, though perhaps simplistic, reason explains his action. In a previous session of Congress, he had sponsored a measure to survey Paducah as a possible site for a naval armaments plant. As a good congressman he had striven to help his district, and as a realistic politician he had sought to increase his ability to dispense patronage. The Naval Affairs Committee, however, had squashed Barkley's initiative. Thus one can easily imagine the Kentucky congressman's opinion of any bill, even one for appropriations, that concerned the navy.

Spite, though, was not one of Barkley's prominent defects. His liberal views overshadowed whatever part vindictiveness played in his less-than-sparkling enthusiasm for preparedness in 1915. He realized that monies spent for military programs detracted from social needs. The mixture of his ambition, his instinctive sympathy for the workingman, and his reverence for Wilson led him toward his own brand of fully developed progressivism. Once Barkley accepted the idea that governmental resources could be used to build roads, buy ships, or check the advance of business monopoly, he pragmatically extended his position to seek governmental solutions to people's problems. Thus he also became, in essence, a nationalist. Obviously he was not a jingo who worked to increase America's prestige and power through imperial expansion and military might. Rather Barkley's posture added to nationalism a different connotation—that of the United States government's responsibility for the welfare of its people.

The finest example of Barkley's combination of progressivism and nationalism appeared in the debates over the Keating-Owen Child Labor Act of 1916. This legislation banned from interstate commerce those goods manufactured by the labor of children under sixteen years of age. American labor leaders and reformers had contrived for years to pass state laws to restrict the employment of youth until their lackluster success led them to lobby for a national bill. Detractors argued that the Keating-Owen Act would reduce the power of the states. "I am getting a little tired,"

Barkley said in debate, ". . . of hearing the standpats on both sides of the Chamber hide behind an antiquated interpretation of the doctrine of States rights." Since acts of Congress a decade earlier assured the American people of the purity of foods and drugs shipped across state lines, Congress could also, Barkley reasoned, "regulate and prevent interstate commerce of an article if it endangers some one in its manufacture and production." Congress passed the bill, and President Wilson signed it into law. Unfortunately, the Supreme Court differed with Barkley and his associates over the powers of Congress to restrict child labor, based on its constitutional mandate to regulate interstate commerce. The Keating-Owen Act, though, was only one of many progressive measures approved by Congress in 1916.

These numerous reform acts received the endorsement of President Wilson who strongly desired to be reelected in the fall. Wilson's progressive ardor had cooled visibly after his initial successes in 1913-1914. However, by 1916 he and Democratic strategists agreed that the administration had to resurrect its earlier reform zeal if only to capture the votes of liberal Republicans. Hence an avalanche of bills stamped with the president's blessings poured through Congress to provide such services as a land bank, rural credits, road improvements, and a workmen's compensation law for federal employees. All this activity found Barkley in the thick of the fray—arguing, cajoling, and voting for the spectrum of progressive bills. He was, however, more than a cheerleader for the president's game plan; he believed in these reforms and played a significant part in preparing legislation. His contributions to the Interstate and Foreign Commerce Committee, for example, helped produce the Adamson Act which gave railway workers the eight-hour day. Also, Barkley had promoted prohibition from the moment he entered Congress, and in 1916 he achieved a modicum of success by introducing a bill that would be passed a year later as the Sheppard-Barkley Act. The law inhibited the imbibing of alcoholic drinks by the District of Columbia citizens.

While an impressive array of significant bills added to

Wilson's ammunition for his bid to retain the presidency, Barkley's record as a legislator enabled him to run a pro forma campaign for his own reelection. As was not unusual during these congressional years, other Democrats did not even try to unseat the incumbent First District representative in the primary. And in the general election, the Republican challenger Thomas N. Hazelip, Barkley's old opponent in the race for county judge, lost by a record margin of 14,000 votes, giving Hazelip a reputation for losing that equaled Barkley's for winning. Despite the easy time Barkley had in his campaign he delivered an incredible one hundred plus speeches between the September adjournment of the active Sixty-fourth Congress and the November general election. He reserved his oratorical fireworks to spark the campaigns of other Democrats not only in Kentucky but also in Illinois, Maine, Missouri, and Tennessee. The reputation he secured as an outstanding speaker and party stalwart thus began to extend beyond the Commonwealth's borders. By far, most of Barkley's speeches were delivered in support of the national ticket in the successful effort to re-elect President Wilson.

Barkley and other surrogate speakers for the president used not only the legislative record but also the slogan "he kept us out of war" to gain votes for Wilson in his narrow victory over Republican challenger Charles Evans Hughes. Ironically, decisions in Europe would make a mockery of the peace campaign the Democrats waged after the national convention. The swirl of events and mounting crises between January and April 1917 left Barkley and the American people embittered, confused, angered, shocked—and ready for war.

The new year brought desperate moves by the German government to break the stalemate of trench warfare that had settled over the western front. For example, on February 1 the Germans violated their pledge to the United States by lifting the restrictions against their submarines. The dust had not settled from the explosive wrath of the American press over this issue when the British delivered to the Wilson administration a copy of an intercepted telegram from German Foreign Secretary Arthur Zimmermann to the German minister in Mexico. In it, Zimmermann invited Mexico, in case America entered the war against Germany, to attack the United States in return for money and Mexico's "lost provinces," that is, the several states in America's Southwest. Release of this telegram to the press and the consequent public outcry for war were further punctuated in March by the torpedoing of three American sea transports. The president reluctantly concluded that he and the United States government could protect America's freedom of the seas only by a declaration of war—a request he made to a joint session of Congress on April 2, 1917.

Although concerned with domestic affairs and reluctant to support military measures, Barkley was caught up in the national mood and angered by German actions. Furthermore, he admired profoundly Wilson's leadership in foreign affairs, particularly the president's attempts to bring peace to the European belligerents, efforts the Germans seemed to torpedo, both figuratively and literally. Thus Barkley spoke with chauvinistic fervor against Imperial Germany and in favor of the declaration of war, and on April 16, 1917, he voted with 372 other colleagues in the House of Representatives for the resolution. As if his rhetoric and vote were not enough, the nearly forty-year-old congressman considered resigning from office to enlist in military service. Fortunately, Barkley had the common sense to heed President Wilson's advice to stay at his post in Congress.

Barkley would later see action on the western front even though he remained in Congress. He joined an unofficial congressional delegation that went to Europe near the end of hostilities between August and October 1918. The junket was unusual, for members of the group paid for their own expenses and acted without benefit of any mandate from their peers. Out of curiosity and interest, members of this delegation wanted to see and participate in those events that had influenced their lives and had been the focus of their attentions for well over a year. The group met and talked with the principal political and royal leaders of England, France, Belgium, and Italy and also visited hospitals, prisoner-of-war camps, and even the battlefield. At Ypres American military officers led the group to within twenty-five yards of the German front lines. On a lark, Barkley grabbed a rifle, placed a helmet on the bayonet, and waved it above the muddy trench. Deadly fire from the German lines struck the helmet eleven times before Barkley could withdraw the weapon. That experience and several close calls from German artillery may have convinced him that he had made a wise choice in fighting the war from Capitol Hill.

During hostilities a number of war-related matters engrossed Barkley's interest. He spoke convincingly for the conscription law, endorsed through his vote the war revenue bill, but most importantly kept his finger on the progressive pulse by championing women's suffrage and the prohibition experiment. He authored the Barkley amendment to the Lever Food and Fuel Act, which would have conserved grains by forbidding the use of feeds for producing alcoholic beverages. This legislation appealed both to those reformers who sought sobriety and to those patriots who realized that the poor wheat crop of 1916 mandated preservation of grains for feeds and foods, not spirits. Although the House of Representatives agreed with Barkley, the Senate and subsequent House-Senate conference committee compromised, diluting the amendment. The final draft of the bill approved in August 1917 permitted the manufacture of beers and wines. Nevertheless, Barkley became a national figure of prominence especially among Anti-Saloon League members. After the war, in fact, the congressman and his teetotaling allies succeeded in imposing prohibition on the American people through the Eighteenth Amendment and through legislation implementing that article to the Constitution.

Another matter transcending the war and quilting the fabric of Barkley's endeavors concerned the railroads. The railroads had always been the farmer's nemesis, and the western Kentucky representative could only applaud President Wilson's decision in December 1917 to nationalize the lines. Labor problems and mobilization tangles had created nightmares out of terminals as overburdened lines buried American efficiency underneath unbelievable chaos. The president acted under authority derived from an army appropriations bill, allowing members of Congress to normalize his action and fill in the gaps at their leisure. Barkley, as a member of the Interstate and Foreign Commerce Committee, applied his influence to preparations and advocacy for the Federal Control Act that emerged from Congress's labors in March 1918.

When the war ended the following November, the railroad controversy captured nearly as much attention as the peace negotiations. While the crusade to make the world safe for democracy sputtered at the Paris peace talks, so did the progressive impulse. A reluctance toward foreign entanglements coupled with partisan politics led to the rejection of both the Versailles Peace Treaty and the American participation in the League of Nations. At the same time attitudes at home turned against reforms, and the American people elected a Republican, and generally more conservative, Congress, placing Barkley and his Democratic cohorts in the new and uncomfortable situation of belonging to a minority party. The president, besieged by the problems of peace, abandoned many of his domestic responsibilities; ultimately, he suffered an incapacitating stroke in the fruitless struggle to rouse favorable public opinion for his uncompromising stand on the League of Nations. Among other casualties in this difficult period was a sane and responsible railroad policy.

Initially, Barkley preferred that railroads remain under government control. He liked the plan proposed by the Railroad Administration's Director-General William G. McAdoo to keep the lines under government ownership for a minimum of five years. When President Wilson, however, bent to the wind of opinion and in May 1919 convened a special session of Congress to legislate the railroads' return to private ownership, Barkley resigned himself to the inevitable—working long hours with Republicans to design an equitable bill. The one introduced by John J. Esch naturally went to the Interstate and Foreign Commerce Committee, which, in turn, appointed Barkley in July to a special subcommittee that redrafted the bill. Barkley then supported the measure in debate before the House in November, but unfortunately this version varied substantially from the legislation sponsored in the Senate by Albert B. Cummins. Although Barkley served on the conference committee to iron out the differences between the House and Senate bills, the resulting Esch-Cummins Transportation Act was so onerous to the western Kentuckian that he issued a minority report in February 1920 and proceeded to fight the bill on the floor of the House. Barkley's ire focused on a change in an amendment he had written which originally would have allowed the Interstate Commerce Commission some flexibility in determining equitable railroad rates. The revised statute, though, instructed the commission to fix rates that produced a substantially high 6 percent return on the aggregate value of railroad property. Barkley pleaded in vain that the bill "in effect sets up a favorable class and confers upon them guarantees and safeguards accorded by legislation to no other class."

The railroad squabbles and his progressive instincts prompted Barkley as delegate to the 1920 Democratic convention to support the nomination of McAdoo. However, when dark-horse candidate James M. Cox and his running mate Franklin D. Roosevelt emerged as the party's standard-bearers, the partisan Barkley entered the election campaign circuit once again speaking on behalf of the Democratic ticket. Although in the future Barkley would be linked closely to the name of Roosevelt, his enthusiasm for these Democratic candidates was less than effervescent. He devoted most of his rhetoric to reminding listeners of the reform measures and of the international spirit President Wilson's name evoked. The audiences he spoke to and the American people in general, however, spurned Barkley's advice and voted Republican Warren G. Harding into office.

The new administration drew a mixed reaction from liberal Democrats. Several Republican policies and programs, such as the creation of the Veterans' Bureau, attracted Barkley's favor. In addition, he assumed a position of leadership as the ranking minority member of the Interstate and Foreign Commerce Committee. Finally, he and other progressives achieved some minor victories as in the case of the Sheppard-Towner Maternity Act, which bolstered financially state agencies concerned with needy mothers and their infants. But the previous administration's spark, zest, moral fervor, and concern for business competition and for the people's welfare had vanished. Barkley felt uncomfortable as the new president and Republican leaders showered attention on big business and wealthy Americans, in such forms as high tariffs and regressive income taxes. At a Jefferson-Jackson Day dinner held in Harding's hometown of Marion, Ohio, in January 1922, Barkley finally vented his frustration. He called Republican legislation "tragic" and said that if Republicans had returned America to normalcy, "then in God's name let us have Abnormalcy."

Barkley's restless dissatisfaction with the Harding administration increased dramatically after his own reelection in the fall of 1922. He carried every First District county including the Republican strongholds of Caldwell and Crittenden. With this assurance of tenure in his congressional office, Barkley looked for new challenges. The solid base of his support, the fame he had won for his wit and oratorical skill, and his reputation as a party regular who had avoided intraparty struggles made him one of the most attractive and eligible candidates for statewide office that Kentucky had seen for a generation. And his unspoken drive for higher office subtly colored Barkley's decisions. Over the next four years his assets and ambitions would lead the Paducah politician to gamble and lose the only election in his career but also, and more importantly, to win a prestigious seat in the United States Senate.

3

TALE OF TWO ELECTIONS

ALBEN W. BARKLEY did not have a chance to savor his own victory in the First District congressional race, nor did he allow Kentucky voters the opportunity for a brief respite from political campaigns before he declared on November 11, 1922, that he would be a candidate for the 1923 Kentucky gubernatorial race. Scholars and commentators then and now have examined the Paducah politician's motives in detail, but, barring the unselfish motive of a saintly soul, there remain only two reasons why anyone at anytime would want to undergo the responsibilities and headaches that accompany the single four-year term provided by the state constitution for the Commonwealth's chief executive. The governorship is either a launching pad for higher political office or a rewarding honor to a lengthy political career. (The governorship is not always an honor. Kentucky historian Thomas D. Clark in his book *Kentucky: Land of Contrast* related this story: "One revered old governor told a group of intimate friends at a meeting of the Kentucky Club in Washington that there were two things he never wanted to have again. One was gonorrhea, and the other the governorship of Kentucky.")

Barkley's successful life in politics already had spanned seventeen years in local and national offices, but retirement rarely entered his head then or thereafter. True, he had lost some of his youthful appearance by gaining weight during his congressional years. His girth amply filled his favorite style of double-breasted suits and his new dimensions added to his jowls and squared his oval face. However, only the slightly lighter shades of brown below his neatly trimmed wavy forelocks indicated that Barkley had reached middle age. His hazel eyes and large mouth were quick to smile and quick to charm, but, at the same time, Barkley could set his jaw and with his formidable presence awe the viewer with his determination. And in 1922 Barkley was determined to make a race for the governor's office in order to gain a seat in the United States Senate.

Barkley failed to articulate his ambition and for good reason. The logical time for him to run for the United States Senate would be in 1926 when Republican incumbent Richard P. Ernst from Covington would be up for reelection. If he won the governor's post he would have to campaign for the Senate in midterm, and if he won the Senate seat he would have to vacate the governorship before his full four years were up. While party workers and knowledgeable voters almost expected the governor to use his position as a catapult for higher office, a politician's admitting that he considered the Frankfort office a temporary job would be the kiss of doom on election day. Barkley ignored with telling silence those critics who charged that he entered the 1923 governor's primary only to improve his chances for the 1926 Senate race. Unsuccessful in dodging the attack, several months later the exasperated and worried Barkley responded to the charge with a lengthy, cleverly worded, self-serving, and open-ended answer. He reminded Kentucky voters that "the Senatorship, like the Governorship, belongs to the people. It is theirs to bestow upon whomever they will. I may never ask them to bestow it upon me. But I do not feel that any man, in order to be allowed to perform the service that is at hand, should be required to bar himself from any future service that the people might wish him to perform."

In actual fact the critics were right. Barkley used to good advantage the experience of running for governor to overcome three obstacles to securing a statewide office. First, he lacked an organizational structure beyond the boundaries of his First District counties. Second, in many respects Barkley had better name-recognition among national politicians and interest groups than among potential constituents in central and eastern Kentucky. Although he had espoused issues of interest to reformers, farmers, and workers and had received the plaudits of Democracy for his address before the 1919 state Democratic convention, Barkley had never canvassed the state to prompt the attentions and forge the alliances necessary to conduct a state campaign. The final obstacle the Paducah politician had to overcome was the shambles presented in general by the Democratic party of Kentucky.

The state party that nurtured Barkley has been for a long time the source of amazement, amusement, and bewilderment to students of Kentucky politics. Factional squabbles of the late nineteenth century tumbled into the twentieth century and shaped the strife that marked the distinguishing trait of Kentucky Democracy for years thereafter. The key issue at that earlier date was the impetus for change embodied in the leadership of William Jennings Bryan. Democrats split between conservatives and radicals even after the national party chose Bryan as the Democratic nominee in three presidential elections between 1896 and 1908. The party fights that marred the intervening years resulted in the sordid assassination of one Kentucky governor, the character assassination of most other politicians, the complete destruction of all chances for a genuine populist or progressive government in Kentucky, the steady growth of the Republican party, and the semipermanent factionalization of the Democrats among groups led by onetime governor J. C. W. Beckham and Seventh District Congressman J. Campbell Cantrill.

By the 1920s the factional battles had more to do with power politics than ideological postures between conservative and liberal Democrats. The foundation of Barkley's early successes had been built on the fact that his safe and predominantly Democratic district enabled him to avoid the intraparty fights that occurred mainly in the northeastern section of the state. That area became an unpredictable tinderbox that exploded to destroy Democracy's statewide control. Conservative and monied Democrats of northern and central Kentucky sometimes switched their support to the Republican standard and augmented disproportionately the power of GOP strongholds in south-central and eastern Kentucky. From the Democratic view, the Republicans exchanged with Democrats the two United States Senate seats and the governor's mansion with distressing regularity. For example, when Barkley announced his decision to run for governor, Republican Edwin P. Morrow held that office.

The Beckham faction forced Barkley's hand and made him declare his candidacy before he and the voters of Kentucky were ready for another election battle. In the crusade for prohibition Barkley allowed his name to be loosely identified with that group. Yet Beckham's allies among the metropolitan newspapers of Louisville began a "Business Man for Governor" campaign as early as November 10, 1922, in the *Courier-Journal*. That outburst not only dictated the timing of Barkley's announcement but also shaped the business rhetoric he employed in speeches. The object of the businessman theme was clear, for in the opinion of even neophyte political analysts, by 1922 the only strong contenders were Barkley and Cantrill. By trying to attract voter sympathy for a nonpolitician (or one out of office) to run for governor, the faction had hoped to undercut the contenders and to promote the candidacy of Beckham associate Judge Isaac Thurman or Beckham himself. However, the ploy failed to catch on in Kentucky beyond Louisville, and the followers of Beckham belatedly turned to Barkley at the end of June 1923. As historian George W. Robinson concluded, Beckham's support was more anti-Cantrill than pro-Barkley.

During the interim of nearly eight months, Barkley in essence had to create his own faction in order to make any impression and gain any strength in the eastern half of the state. He never acquired much of a reputation for comprehending the nuts and bolts of political campaigning, particularly in the area of finance. But in the 1923 primary race for governor he demonstrated by his choice of lieutenants an uncommon skill in political craftsmanship. To chair the campaign he selected Louisville lawyer Elwood Hamilton who belonged to Beckham's law firm and carried impeccable credentials for his opposition to Cantrill. At the same time, Barkley was able to secure the services of Wiley B. Bryan, sometime member of Cantrill's camp, to be his treasurer. Finally, he placed his own supporter, Mildred Spaulding, in charge of state headquarters in Louisville.

Despite this organization, if Barkley hoped to win, he had to wrest support from Kentucky areas his opponent knew by instinct not hearsay. Cantrill had been a state senator from Scott County before Barkley had passed his bar examination, and the faction leader had been a seasoned member of the United States House of Representatives before the McCracken County judge ran for the same office in the First District in 1912. The talents of Cantrill had been tested and tempered in the fires of battles that stemmed from the early days of the twentieth century, when he as state senator had welded a group in the legislature that frustrated the will and the program of Governor Beckham. Although Cantrill had earned Beckham's undying wrath and perpetual opposition, he managed to gain reelection to Congress with a consistency few except Barkley equaled.

The solid political successes and reputations Barkley and Cantrill enjoyed inevitably placed them in contention for the 1923 governor's primary. Yet for a decade the pair had been congressional colleagues and each respected the other. In addition, the move Beckham's forces made to destroy the aspirations and designs of both Barkley and Cantrill fused them temporarily into an unholy alliance by their mutual distrust of the man who propagated for his own ends the "Business Man for Governor" campaign. Before the end of 1922, Barkley and Cantrill agreed not to employ personal invective or abuse to achieve a primary victory. Although their lieutenants slung enough dirt to cover both men in a mountain of mud, the principal candidates kept their word and turned the election into one of the most refreshing and issue-oriented affairs ever experienced by Kentucky voters.

Barkley did not even mention Cantrill's name when the former opened his campaign in historic Danville, on Monday, February 19, 1923. Significantly the community is located geographically near the center of the state and Barkley's choice of city for his initial speech reflected accurately his need and desire to garner Democratic votes in that area and merge this support with his considerable base of power in the western part of the state. The platform he articulated there, with one exception, became the basis for all his future speeches. And if one can believe the rhetoric Barkley used in his soft country accent, reinforced by the clenched right fist and characteristically cocked elbow flailing through the air, salvation from Kentucky's ills was close at hand.

Barkley advocated changing and consolidating elections so that Kentucky citizens would not be assaulted by politicians every year. The Paducah orator also expressed his fears over the rise in crime and became a law-and-order candidate. He called for a conservation policy and he favored, not unforeseeably, the immediate completion of Kentucky's highway network. If elected, he promised to create a nonpartisan highway commission composed of full-time paid members. He pointed out that he was a farmer's son and stated he would appoint at least one farmer to every board "which has to do with the assessment, collection or expenditure of public funds." Deploring Kentucky's low-ranking among the states in fostering public education, he made specific remarks on reorganizing the state system and upgrading higher education. But if one theme permeated his list and gave coherence to his solutions for Kentucky's problems, it was the idea of efficiency. Barkley was at his best in denouncing the alleged greed, graft, and favoritism evidenced by the current Republican regime. He wanted to reduce the state debt and eliminate the "extravagance, waste, duplication . . . by the application of rigid business methods to the business affairs of the state." Thus in every issue that touched Barkley's interest he confounded the Beckham faction's "Business Man for Governor" gambit by becoming the businessman's businessman.

Barkley's audience could applaud warmly and nod approvingly as they listened to his soothing and appealing platform shaped by his long-held beliefs, but which also contained a number of last-minute platitudes. What grabbed the listeners' interest and caught the readers' eye in the next day's newspapers was his apparent attack on Kentucky coal-mine operators. Barkley lamented Republican inefficiency but he also recognized that some increase in government expenditures could not be avoided. What goaded the congressional representative was that revenues were raised through the property tax which hurt particularly the small farmer and property owner. In typical Barkley fashion he amassed and presented with meticulous care his statistics. He pointed out that the state produced $160 million in coal in 1922. "Eighty-eight per cent of this coal," he went on, "found its market in other states, and it is a singular fact that this amount . . . was greater than the total assessed valuation of all the coal property in Kentucky for that same year." Barkley thought that a tonnage tax would be a game-winning triple play. In his mind such a coal tax would reduce property taxes, acquire new revenues paid mainly by out-of-state buyers, and force coal interests to carry their fair share of the tax burden.

After Barkley fought the coal lobby obliquely, and sometimes openly, he later added the powerful Kentucky Jockey Club to his list of opponents. In a speech delivered at Lebanon, Kentucky, on April 2, he came out foursquare against gambling on horses. "If it is immoral to shoot dice, or play poker, or roll a roulette wheel, what is it," he asked logically, "that sanctifies a race track?" The ailing Cantrill could not have been more pleased with the witch's brew Barkley stirred for himself. Cantrill's campaign coffer grew in direct proportion to each speech Barkley made against the coal and racetrack lobbies. Yet quite admirably the western Kentuckian jumped to the offensive, demonstrated raw courage, and provided voters with a liberal program that clearly separated him from his opponent. It would be an understatement to say Barkley grabbed the voters' attention by his unorthodox views on pari-mutuel betting and mining in a state noted for horses and coal.

Barkley's canvass of the state shifted into high gear during the summer months, but with predictable and unwelcomed results. The inveterate campaigner used an automobile and pushed the wheezing, coughing vehicle to the limits by driving day-long jaunts on imperfect highways and stopping at every town to deliver a speech. Newspaper correspondents gasped at Barkley's pace and sometimes failed to find the strength and perseverance to match his stamina. Amazed by Barkley's durability, the journalists began to tag him with the label "Iron Man." Living up to his reputation, the "Iron Man" survived his car which two days before the August 4 primary shuddered and sputtered its last. If effort alone could determine a winner, Barkley should have walked off with first prize. However, he lost and by the relatively narrow margin of less than 10,000 votes. In an astounding demonstration of geopolitical cleavage, Barkley and Cantrill won respectively the western and eastern halves of the state. The key to Barkley's loss was in the heavily populated urban areas—Lexington, Louisville, and Frankfort—where Cantrill amassed 75 or more percent of the votes. Barkley simply could not overcome the controversies he stirred and the organization Cantrill displayed in the eastern urban areas of the Commonwealth.

Three days after Cantrill's victory, Barkley pledged his support to the victor in the general election. This magnanimous gesture gained for him the deepest respect in the camp of his former opponent. Although Cantrill won the primary and secured the allegiances of his adversary, he lost prematurely life's battle with death on September 2, 1923, after he failed to recover from an earlier abdominal operation. Members of the Democratic State Central Committee which met on September 11 might have endorsed the primary's runner-up had Barkley not proclaimed his refusal to accept a nomination from a committee rather than from the voters. The committee picked instead Cantrill's conservative congressional associate William J. Fields ("Honest Bill from Olive Hill") as the party's nominee and Barkley proceeded immediately to campaign and aid Fields's successful bid for the governor's chair in the fall election. In essence, Barkley's actions following the primary, dictated partly by ambition and partly by his philosophy of party, turned his narrow and only defeat into a political debit he would collect with interest three years later. Added to his considerable vote-getting appeal among farmers and reformers would be Cantrill's organization and the sympathy of all Democrats who aspired to achieve party unity.

While Barkley received the applause of most Democrats and strengthened his hand for the future, his personal finances restricted his options. He had spent considerable sums amounting to several thousand dollars of his personal funds in the close primary race. Whatever ultimate goal he possessed, by the end of the primary campaign trail his commitment in time and money etched in his memory the election's loss as a sincere disappointment. In addition to funding his campaign, he invested whatever loose change he could find in a variety of oil schemes at a time when declining petroleum prices guaranteed misery for the hapless investor. Finally, Barkley had earned substantial gratuities by demonstrating his oratorical skills in the cause of preserving prohibition. By 1923, though, his ardor and the number of his speeches had declined. Prohibition had been a progressive reform. However, the rise of organized crime and the incrimination of those American millions who refused to refrain from consuming alcoholic drinks turned the national experiment on its ear and raised more and graver moral issues than those intended to be solved by the Eighteenth Amendment.

Whatever his situation, Barkley's financial weaknesses alone prevented him from engaging in any major statewide political activity for several years. In 1924 Democratic Senator Augustus Owsley Stanley was up for reelection. He had managed one way or another to alienate every major Democratic group in the state. Not only had he alarmed Barkley's reformist friends by criticizing vociferously the anti-alcoholic experiment, but earlier as governor (1915-1919) Stanley had acquired the permanent enmity of conservative, racist, and ultrapatriotic individuals by supporting anti-lynching laws and by vetoing a wartime bill that would have prohibited the teaching of German in the public schools. The capstone to Stanley's fall from Democracy's grace occurred in his initial opposition to the nomination of Fields for governor. Small wonder Barkley's name loomed up with regularity in the press and among those disenchanted party workers who hoped to find a stronger Democrat to replace the unpopular senator. Barkley's financial condition, however, made him indicate early in 1924 that he could not run against Stanley in the next primary. Also, Barkley had stored such a treasure trove of goodwill by his behavior after the 1923 primary and by his promotion of an image as a party unifier that it seemed contradictory at best to challenge an incumbent Democrat—something he had done only once in his life when he ran for county attorney in 1905. Better to wait, Barkley reasoned, for 1926 when he would be the obvious candidate to oppose Republican Ernst than to destroy party harmony by a premature bid for the Senate seat.

Although Barkley kept a lower profile in state politics and allowed time to ripen his ambitions, he remained active in national politics as congressman and as delegate to the 1924 national convention in New York. Republican President Warren G. Harding died the previous year and Calvin Coolidge found himself, through one of the accidents of history, elevated to the nation's top post. Despite the Harding administration's legacy of scandal and corruption, Coolidge coupled prosperity to his untainted reputation to become the logical choice for his party's nomination. Meanwhile, Barkley joined the Democrats at Madison Square Garden amidst initial and justified optimism. The party of Jefferson, Jackson, and Wilson had rebounded in 1922 from earlier defeats to cut the opposition majority in the Senate to eight and in the House of Representatives to eighteen. Republican scandals added a bright touch to Democratic hopes, when deliberations began on June 24, that they might be able to elect a president.

As in 1920, Barkley and rural Democrats wanted Wilson's heir apparent William G. McAdoo to be their nominee. Urban party leaders under the additional impetus of the convention's location voted consistently for their candidate, New York governor Alfred E. Smith. The Democratic split ended in protracted voting, and from Barkley's vantage point the only positive gain from the long heated sessions was that convention chairman Thomas J. Walsh surrendered temporarily his gavel to the western Kentuckian in order to acquire a brief rest from the chair's ordeal. After 103 ballots the Democrats had frittered away their optimism among themselves, their credibility among the American people, and their patience with each other—at one exasperating moment when Barkley chaired the session his noted humor and country grace yielded to a four-letter expletive. When McAdoo and Smith withdrew their names, the convention selected a competent nonentity, John W. Davis, to head the party's ticket and Barkley witnessed the destruction of Democratic power on the national level that was agonizingly similar to what he had experienced in Kentucky. Though Barkley defeated his Republican challenger by a two-to-one margin and retained his congressional seat, the factionalization of the party on the national level led to a Republican president and on the state level to a Republican senator, Frederick M. Sackett. The lesson these events brought home to Barkley led him to be almost paranoiac on the topic of party unity.

To avoid disrupting the harmony his name summoned among Kentucky Democratic factions, Barkley refrained from asserting his influence in state politics though he had numerous opportunities and requests to do so in the period between 1924 and 1926. He amply filled his time with congressional affairs—in particular his attentions fell on a problem that returned with the regularity of an old but irritating acquaintance. Early in 1924 Barkley cosponsored another railroad bill. He had never been pleased with the Esch-Cummins Transportation Act and his displeasure mounted with the bitter 1922 railroad disputes. What raised his concern was the semibinding decisions of the Railroad Labor Board whose members in adjudicating conflicts between labor and management generally sided with management. Barkley wanted an impartial board that would mediate quarrels without impairing entirely the railroad brotherhoods' use of the strike or the threat of a strike to improve wages and working conditions. Although Republican opponents delayed its course and Barkley had to surrender his sponsorship to get it passed, the Railway Labor Act of 1926 created the United States Board of Mediation and contained the substance of Barkley's ideas. The bill augmented his legislative reputation in and out of Congress and made him something of a folk hero among members of the labor movement.

Not unexpectedly the Associated Railway Labor Organizations endorsed Barkley's candidacy for the United States Senate a month before he announced his intentions on April 23, 1926. Barkley's delay in making a formal bid for office was not his typical style, but the struggle he had endured in 1923 made him desire a clear field for the Democratic nomination and he wanted to see what kind of opposition might form within his own party before he declared his candidacy. That no other candidate could raise the interest of any Democratic faction indicated the care Barkley had exerted in 1923 to prepare for the 1926 campaign and the wisdom he had demonstrated in avoiding party conflicts between 1923 and 1926.

Thus after the filing date had passed at the end of June 1926 and Barkley was the only Democrat entered, he could concentrate on building an organization that would challenge Republican Senator Richard P. Ernst. For campaign manager Barkley chose Congressman Fred M. Vinson, the future chief justice of the Supreme Court (1946-1953). Vinson's main asset in 1926, though, was his reputation for being able to get along with Kentucky coal-mine owners. Barkley's concern to pacify the coal operators and horse-racing enthusiasts whose ire he had raised in his gubernatorial campaign, while smart politics, was not necessary. Coal-mine owners and Kentucky Jockey Club members quietly supported Barkley's campaign in order to keep the reformer out of the state and to prevent him from running for governor in 1927. Finally, the politician had anticipated his need for funds by raising cash from national party sources such as New York financier Bernard Baruch.

With his finances and organization established, Barkley bought another car and toured the state with his daughter Laura Louise in the summer. This initial canvass of the state was quite unlike his gubernatorial efforts, for the campaign would not really get under way until September and instead of making a large number of public speeches, he conferred with local party leaders, particularly in the eastern half of the state, to build the necessary structure for his fall campaign. Despite this difference, the "Iron Man" literally drove himself too hard. On several occasions on the road, Laura Louise had to startle her drowsy father by shouting "Ernst!" in Barkley's ear.

Significantly Barkley opened the public campaign in Paris on September 11. Seat of Bourbon County, Paris was in the center of Kentucky's horse-farm country and of Cantrill's followers. His earlier talks with county Democrats assured a large crowd for his first major speech. Barkley used much of his invective to abuse Republican programs rather than his opponent. He attacked the protective tariff, regressive taxes, excessive expenditures, and economic strife among Kentucky farmers that had been caused by Republican policy or insensitivity. Reserved for Ernst was Barkley's hostile criticism that the Republican was morally culpable if not actually corrupt. Unfortunately for Ernst the charge had some truth, for Ernst had voted to exonerate and later seat a Republican senator from Michigan who had been convicted of electoral improprieties.

Ernst began his canvass for reelection at the end of September. The Republican relied on Coolidge prosperity and the slogan "Coolidge Needs Ernst" to gain his votes. Most farmers, however, had overextended during World War I and when Europe recovered after the conflict, Kentucky and American farmers would soon face a decade of declining prices, mortgage foreclosures, overproduction, and an economic depression which began long before the Wall Street crash of 1929. Also, factory workers did not receive their fair share in wages from the value of the goods their labor produced. So the phrase "Coolidge prosperity" did not apply to all the members of Kentucky's electorate and was at best a mixed blessing for the Republican cause. In addition, Ernst made mistakes, the kind that lose votes. For example, he opposed the Barkley-supported soldiers' bonus for World War I veterans. Finally, Barkley converted the slogan "Coolidge Needs Ernst" into a joke. "If Coolidge needs Ernst," Barkley bubbled, "it is proof enough that Kentucky does not need him."

In the period before the November election, Barkley delivered up to a dozen speeches and drove over a hundred miles per day. His tremendous pace and aggressive campaign resurrected his 1923 label, "Iron Man." While most of his efforts were directed toward the eastern half of the state, his care in preparing for the canvass and his avoidance of error led to victory. The final tally placed him ahead of Ernst by the relatively small margin of 20,000 votes, yet in beating the incumbent, always a difficult task politically, Barkley managed to usurp from the Republicans twenty-three counties that they had carried two years earlier. While Barkley believed that, on the hustings or in the Congress, party unity spelled success, his victory was actually a personal tribute. Barkley had unified the party behind his candidacy, but the evident cohesion of 1926 would crumble within a year. The knack he possessed to conciliate factions and ingratiate himself among potential opponents would serve him well as a distinguished representative from Kentucky to the United States Senate.

4

TRANSITIONS
AND TROUBLED TIMES

ALBEN W. BARKLEY was still Kentucky's First District congressman in the United States House of Representatives when he returned to Washington, D.C., a month after his election to the United States Senate. Not until the opening of the Seventieth Congress in December 1927 would Barkley move into the Senate chamber. Meanwhile he would exist in a state of near political limbo for a year—maintaining haphazard interest in House affairs while eagerly awaiting his new position in the Senate. The lame-duck Sixty-ninth Congress lived up to the reputation earned by previous postelection legislative sessions. Holdover pieces of legislation were debated with diminished enthusiasm while defeated members pondered their future, victorious congressmen celebrated their fortune, and political leaders calculated the relative strengths and weaknesses of the upcoming Congress. In the interim one of the few measures that captured Barkley's interest was a bill that provided for the construction of a bridge across the Ohio River at Paducah. His support for this important expansion of Paducah's commercial and cultural life marked an appropriate end to Barkley's years in the House of Representatives, for through this bill he could repay the city that had nourished his political career.

The uninspired finish to the Sixty-ninth Congress contrasted sharply with the lively start of the Seventieth. Although Democratic members of the United States Senate faced a Republican majority of two, the whims of old progressive or insurgent Republicans guaranteed excitement and made a mockery of GOP dominance except on the initial vote that organized the Senate under Republican leadership. Barkley found himself assigned to the Senate's Library, Finance, Banking and Currency, and, later, to the Interstate Commerce committees. These committees, important in any period, would assume special significance in time of depression and place the senator from Paducah in the midst of the maelstrom of America's ills when the economic crash occurred two years later. Naturally, except for an occasional prescient observer or a lucky prophet of doom, most Americans remained blissfully ignorant of their dreadful future.

While the new Congress undertook to organize its affairs and appointed recently elected representatives and senators to committee vacancies, the presidential election of 1928 weighed heavily upon the minds and actions of everyone in Washington. For several reasons, Barkley felt a sense of urgency to the presidential selection process. In the spring of 1928, Vice President Charles G. Dawes in his capacity as the Senate's presiding officer appointed Barkley to a special committee chaired by Republican Senator Frederick Steiwer to investigate the campaign expenditures of leading presidential hopefuls. These included Democrat Alfred E. Smith and Republican Herbert Hoover, Coolidge's high-powered, strong-willed commerce secretary.

Far more important than this inquiry was the fact that Barkley's name emerged for the first time among Democrats who felt he might do well in the first or second place on the presidential ticket. Barkley's dark-horse candidacy arose from the fame he had gained as a staunch wheelhorse and party regular who had espoused and sponsored prominent legislation that appealed to a broad spectrum of American farmers, workers, and reformers. Barkley had used the lengthy interim between the Sixty-ninth and Seventieth congresses to augment his farm support by making a number of speeches before regional agricultural groups. In addition, as a border-state politician, the Kentucky senator could become a compromise candidate or balance a ticket led by an urban politician. He already possessed, despite his reduced enthusiasm for prohibition, the endorsement of the Anti-Saloon League as one of several politicians that body favored for the presidency. Finally, Barkley's gregarious charm and soothing personality molded neatly into the pattern of conciliation sought by many Democrats who remembered the divisive and disastrous 1924 convention.

Ironically, although Barkley identified himself with those who worked for party harmony, the titular head of Kentucky Democracy faced a state party once again divided into clear-cut factions. The 1927 gubernatorial race had reopened old wounds. This time J. C. W. Beckham did not bother with a surreptitious "Business Man for Governor" ploy, but came out swinging for the Democratic nomination. When the old J. Campbell Cantrill faction, now led by Louisville banker and publisher James B. Brown and Governor William J. Fields, failed to check Beckham's progress toward the nomination, many faction members openly or secretly bolted the party in the victorious move to elect Republican Flem D. Samson. At the same time the rest of the Democrats defeated their Republican counterparts on the state ticket. Following the campaign, Beckham's forces demanded the exclusion of the "bolters" from the party and for a time it seemed likely that Kentucky Democrats might split into two irreconcilable factions.

Since Barkley was not up for reelection until 1932, his normal concern for party unity was genuine, albeit remote. After his performance in the 1923 and 1926 elections, his name alone brought votes from the opposing factions. However, 1928 was not a normal year. His unarticulated hopes to leave his options open for higher office prompted his appearance at the April meeting of the Democratic State Executive Committee. He expressed the unity theme, but he pursued the establishment of a power base to meet future possibilities raised by the upcoming national party convention. Barkley continued to push for reconciliation in the spring of 1928 and delivered the keynote address on the same topic before the mid-June convocation of the state convention. Party realists who grasped the dangers presented by any move to excommunicate party bolters joined Barkley in approving a compromise that excluded only those Democrats who had campaigned actively for a Republican candidate. This patchwork truce enabled Kentucky's delegates to proceed by train to the Democratic National Convention in Houston on June 24 under the guise of a consolidated state party.

As the train sped toward Texas, important decisions were made among members of Kentucky's delegation when they divided convention chores among themselves. Barkley surrendered his position as chairman of the delegation to Lieutenant Governor James Breathitt. Coincidently the senator succumbed to the preconvention publicity he had received and to the urgings of Breathitt and Fred Vinson to campaign openly for the vice-presidential nomination. Before the train steamed into Houston on June 25, a public announcement disclosed Barkley's decision.

As soon as the Kentucky delegation was settled in Houston's Rice Hotel, a group of them decided to make a pitch for Barkley's candidacy to those supporting the leading contender for the Democratic presidential nomination, Alfred E. Smith. Although pleased by the reception they received from Smith's lieutenants, Kentucky's delegates gained no assurances. They knew, however, that Barkley's strong qualifications would balance a ticket led by Smith. The latter was East Coast, urban, Catholic, and anti-prohibitionist while Barkley was border state, rural, Protestant, and proponent of the national anti-alcoholic law. If any factor clouded the equilibrium presented by a ticket of Smith and Barkley, it lay in people's perception of both men as liberals.

In fact, in the opinion of the Smith camp, a Smith-Barkley ticket seemed too balanced. Party intellectuals and knowledgeable voters might revolt against an obviously contrived team that merged two individuals with such diametrically opposed views on the Eighteenth Amendment to the Constitution. As Barkley's friends proceeded to decorate the halls and lobby of the Rice Hotel with placards and posters that proclaimed "Al and Al" and "Embark with Barkley," Smith decided to choose Senator Joseph T. Robinson of Arkansas as his prospective running mate. Robinson possessed many of Barkley's attributes without his jarring publicity and liberal flair.

Naturally, Smith and his associates neglected to inform Barkley and his friends of this decision. The art of politics tended to eliminate candor from convention procedures. Smith, by dangling the vice-presidential nomination before Barkley and the Kentucky delegates, secured the support of a group of energetic men who proceeded to lobby and garner convention votes for Smith's cause. Perhaps to placate his anticipated disappointment, Smith asked Barkley to write and deliver a seconding speech. Thus, at a crucial moment in his own career, Barkley was locked in his room pouring arduously over his speech. There is an element of high tragedy in the whole affair, an element that would be repeated in Barkley's life. He seemed incapable of drawing together the strings that controlled his fate. It was admirable but unrealistic for Barkley to assume that he could be selected for one of the nation's top posts as the reluctant candidate who would be drafted for the honor and not from his own maneuverings. The Smith camp spared itself the embarrassment of seeing and dealing with Barkley.

Barkley delivered his seconding remarks on June 28. The speech not only praised Smith; it excoriated Republicans. With clenched fist and raised voice, Barkley mixed metaphors to remind his audience of the scandals that plagued the GOP era. "In the past eight years," he waxed enthusiastically, "we have witnessed in the United States of America a series of political crimes so nauseating and revolting as to make grand larceny sound like an announcement of a hymn or golden text at a Sunday school." Moreover in key sections of his speech, he attempted to neutralize those controversial aspects to Smith's candidacy, the governor's Roman Catholic religion and his sympathetic view toward ending prohibition. Hence Barkley belabored the Constitution's religious guarantees and pointed to that "dry" plank in the party platform which upheld the Eighteenth Amendment.

Smith was grateful for Barkley's eloquence, but the only recompense he returned was an appreciative telegram. If Barkley had hoped that his seconding speech would prompt a more substantial reward from Smith, these hopes were dashed after Smith won the nomination and announced Robinson as his running mate. However, the Kentucky delegation remained loyal to Barkley and placed his name in nomination. As is usual in such affairs, the presidential nominee's preference prevailed and Robinson took an overwhelming percentage of the vote. What occurred next reflected well on Barkley and indicated clearly the impact his struggles for party harmony had had on his outlook. He strode to the rostrum and changed Kentucky's votes to Robinson's side of the tally in an attempt to make Robinson the unanimous choice of the convention.

At the close of the convention, Alben and Dorothy took an extended voyage from East Coast to West Coast via the Panama Canal. However, like an irritating habit, Smith hovered over the course of Barkley's immediate future. When he concluded his vacation in August 1928, Barkley discovered that in his absence he had been named state chairman for the Smith campaign. His "good fortune" stemmed from his seconding speech and his ability to move with ease among all the diverse elements in Kentucky's Democratic party.

The appointment, though, was a mixed blessing. Barkley's forte lay in the good effect he had by his physical presence and oratorical skills on those he met. By going to Louisville early in September and establishing a state headquarters for Smith, Barkley surrendered his ability to campaign directly for Smith either in Kentucky or in neighboring states. In addition, promoting an urban, Catholic, and "wet" presidential nominee among predominantly rural, Protestant, and "dry" Kentucky voters proved to be a thankless and impossible task. Even the Barkley-arranged October campaign stop by Smith in Louisville and Hodgenville on the thirteenth and fourteenth could not dispel the alienation of the vast majority of the Commonwealth's citizens by Smith's views, religion, and grating East Side New York accent. Barkley tried unsuccessfully to neutralize the statewide bigotry against Smith's campaign which aided the Republican cause. Worst of all, many Democrats clamored publicly for the election of the Republican national ticket headed by Commerce Secretary Herbert Hoover.

Hoover captured 59 percent of the vote in Kentucky, but Smith's drubbing did not discredit Barkley's efforts, for Democracy's loss in Kentucky typified the trend in the nation. And the election was not as close as the percentages would indicate. Smith lost not only three border states but also five traditionally Democratic states in the South. Hoover smothered his opponent by grabbing 444 electoral votes to Smith's 87. Little wonder that on Inauguration Day in March 1929, Hoover permitted himself the luxury of an ebullient and optimistic remark that revealed more about his election victory than the state of the nation. "I have no fears for the future of our country," the new president stated as he pursed his lips into an almost perceptible smile. "It is bright with hope."

Events would soon turn Hoover's words into a phrase of derision. Americans had gone on a buying binge that had raised inflated prices on watered-down stocks sold on Wall Street and had made the whole credit structure as solid as worm-eaten wood. The president himself understood that parts of the economy contradicted the very optimism he expressed. Agriculture had suffered a terrible and continual depression throughout the 1920s. Even though Hoover had decided to make the federal government more efficient and less powerful in its governing role, he called a special session of Congress to provide some aid for the farm industry.

Barkley and other members of Congress had worked perennially to pass legislation to relieve farm distress, but the several Republican administrations and their conservative legislative cohorts had frustrated these efforts. Now Hoover proposed two measures for Congress to consider when the special session opened in mid-April 1929. First, the president wanted an agricultural marketing bill that would establish a federal farm board which in turn would dispense modest sums of money to improve the marketing activities of several farm cooperative organizations. It was the type of indirect patchwork palliative that Barkley found disgusting. He criticized the Agricultural Marketing Act, which was subsequently passed, while simultaneously pushing unsuccessfully for a debenture plan that would have subsidized farm exports and, through a circuitous route, have provided farmers with needed cash. Second, Hoover thought the farmer's ills could best be solved by protecting American agricultural goods through higher tariff rates. The president inadvertently opened Pandora's box, for Congress did not restrict itself to farm products but decided to write a new tariff bill. Barkley believed that higher tariffs hurt the farmer. He soon became a Senate leader of a coalition among liberal Democrats and progressive Republicans who sought to restrain the impetus toward higher rates which Congress revealed in the debates that absorbed a gargantuan portion of legislative time between the late spring of 1929 and June 1930.

During the summer and fall of 1929, Barkley's endeavors in the Finance Committee and on the Senate floor seemed to pay off. But on October 23 securities prices fell sharply on the Stock Exchange. Despite the shoring up provided by a pool of New York bankers and the reassuring words of President Hoover, the drop in prices continued unabated. Within a month stocks lost over $26 billion of their face value. As the spiral of decline set in, bankers and businessmen joined brokers in closing their doors. A new insecurity crept, then rushed, over the land, and Barkley's former allies began to search frantically for an easy way to halt the mood of despair and the collapse of the economy. Members of Congress embraced the concept of a high protective tariff to aid industry and maintain employment.

Barkley argued in vain that a high tariff destroyed foreign trade and hence American jobs. He scorned those colleagues who claimed that a high tariff would benefit farmers. "For every dollar," Barkley blurted angrily, "we have added to the farmer's income by any provision of the tariff bill we have taken ten dollars out of his pocket." And some of this protection, particularly on farm products, appeared downright wrong if not outrightly insane. High duties on sugar, for example, protected a few growers to the detriment of millions of consumers. In addition, exorbitant rates would exclude such items as cornstarch and bananas, although the former entered the country in minute quantities. As for the latter, "If we can shut out bananas," Barkley remarked in debate, "it will require us to eat apples and we will have to change the old adage so that it will be said hereafter . . . 'An apple a day will keep a banana away.' " No amount of Barkley rhetoric or ridicule could shame or persuade the Senate to accept his views. On June 17, 1930, President Hoover signed into law the Hawley-Smoot Tariff. Unfortunately for the nation's economy, Barkley's predictions proved largely accurate. The jerry-built law burdened imports with an average tax of 50 percent that forced other nations to retaliate and severely curtailed America's overseas commerce.

Shortly after the tariff fight, Congress adjourned. To relax, Barkley booked a cabin on a passenger ship and enjoyed a pleasant ocean voyage to England. He arrived in the British Isles in mid-July and attended a session of the Interparliamentary Union. If Barkley had hoped his trip abroad would relieve him of the depression problems, his aspirations proved unfounded. With one exception, all the major countries of Europe were being strangled by the Gordian knot of the economic crash. And that exception, the Soviet Union, for a brief time, would become the center of Barkley's interest. In August 1930 he joined a Soviet tour of thirty Americans led by impressario and publicist Sherwood

Eddy and including such political associates as Senators Burton K. Wheeler and Bronson Cutting.

The tour entered Moscow on August 11. The Soviet capital's feverish commercial activity contrasted sharply with the sluggish economies of the Western world. Soviet Russia was forging ahead through a series of five-year plans which rapidly industrialized a nation that had been tortured by war, revolution, civil war, and famine. The Soviet experiment elevated and exalted state planning as an alternative approach to the fumbling efforts of capitalist nations to deal effectively with the depression. Later reflections on the Soviet experience would balance the genuine industrial progress of the USSR against the terribly inhuman exactions and sacrifices such progress demanded. But in 1930 the Soviet Union gained the grudging respect if not the high admiration of many western politicians including Kentucky's senator.

Barkley and his tour companions shared prepackaged excursions to sights of interest in Moscow and Leningrad. Although he failed to meet the procrustean dictator Joseph Stalin, Barkley had the opportunity to hear briefings by Soviet leaders in education, trade, and planning. At one point he and several of the tour's politicians broke away from the larger group and rented two Model-T Fords plus Russian drivers and took off for some rural villages and collective farms. Barkley barely concealed his exuberance upon leaving the metropolitan areas for the Russian countryside. As if he were campaigning once again for county attorney back in Paducah, Barkley shed his coat, rolled up his sleeves, and joined the common Russian laborers in threshing wheat or cutting logs. Differences in language and the fact that the United States government had not officially recognized Communist Russia (and would not do so until 1933) did not block the empathy Barkley felt for those Russians who toiled on the land.

The warm feeling this excursion left in Barkley remained with him after he returned to the United States early in September. However, he refrained from joining the growing chorus of liberal spokesmen in and out of Congress who called for diplomatic relations and closer ties with Soviet Russia. Unlike the Soviet government, Barkley lacked a glib ideology and master plan to solve economic ills, but he had been impressed by the stark comparison between America and Soviet Russia. "The Russian experiment," Barkley concluded prophetically in a subsequent speech, "will be watched with the greatest interest in every civilized country. Its failure or its success will have a tremendous influence upon the future course of history."

Although Barkley tended to be a fiscal conservative, his Russian trip seemed to make him more aggressive and less patient with the Hoover administration. In his own mind, Barkley indicted the president on three counts for being impervious during the winter session of Congress to the nation's distress. First, Hoover vetoed a Barkley-supported measure that would have allowed veterans to borrow in advance a percentage of bonus money they would receive in 1945. Second, Hoover's apparently insensitive response to the 1930 drought appalled the senator. Only reluctantly, the president signed into law a bill that released a mere $45 million in loans to aid farmers. According to historian Robert F. Sexton, the drought had destroyed farm crops worth twice that amount in Kentucky alone. Third, in the late winter of 1931, Barkley was astounded by Hoover's resolve not to call a special session of Congress. Thus while the American people had been struck by the worst economic calamity and then crushed by the worst crop disaster in their history, Hoover crippled the government's power of response by allowing Congress to have its usual nine-month vacation.

Senator Barkley had planned to be as active in between sessions of Congress as President Hoover was inactive. After a rest with his family in their Paducah home, he set out in June for his Washington office where he hoped to prepare for a number of speeches to be delivered before a variety of organizations. However, on June 22 near Parkersburg, West Virginia, the senator's car went out of control as it slid over

59

loose gravel and hit a telephone pole. Thrown from the car and lucky to survive, Barkley suffered multiple cuts, bruises, and fractures. Treated at length at the Parkersburg hospital, Barkley returned to Paducah to convalesce. His fractures, particularly his damaged right knee, required considerable time to heal in the summer and fall of 1931.

While Barkley experienced this physical setback, the nation's economy sagged even further. The country's situation had plummeted at such an alarming rate that by the time Barkley and other members of Congress returned to Washington in December 1931, Hoover abandoned some of his principles that favored voluntary measures to stem the tide of depression. Congress approved funds for loans that would delay mortgage foreclosures, but the premier bill passed in January 1932 was the Reconstruction Finance Corporation (RFC). A high-powered agency, the RFC made multimillion-dollar loans available to large banks, businesses, and railroads. Despite this effort, Hoover could not escape the criticism that he had provided a breadline for financiers while workers and farmers starved. The RFC was too little, too late. Barkley reflected the views of many contemporaries when he stated on the Senate floor: "We are now dealing only with temporary expedients, only with palliatives, only with sugar-coated pills, which may keep the patient alive until somebody will have enough vision and statesmanship to deal with this question from a fundamental standpoint."

Barkley did not possess such a basic plan and the presidential veto plus a divided Congress prevented progressive politicians from implementing some programs for more substantial relief. But a man who thought he might be able to do something for the country's ills announced his candidacy for the Democratic presidential nomination in January 1932. Barkley reacted benignly to Franklin Delano Roosevelt's plans. The Kentucky senator had known the Hyde Park scion for a generation. Roosevelt had been President Wilson's assistant secretary of the navy and the unlucky vice-presidential candidate for the Democrats in 1920. Much to the plaudits of Barkley and other well-wishers, neither the 1920 loss nor a severe case of polio crippled FDR enough to prevent his replacing Al Smith as governor of New York in 1928 and assuming Smith's mantle as titular leader of the party in 1932.

Although Barkley favored Governor Roosevelt, he refrained from making a public commitment. The Kentucky senator had to be cautious. No Commonwealth representative to the upper house of Congress had secured reelection in the twentieth century. A premature endorsement of a presidential candidate who might be out of touch with the wishes of Kentucky's electorate could seriously disturb the delicate balance which Barkley had achieved among the Commonwealth's Democrats. On the other hand, Roosevelt made no secret of his need for Barkley's border-state support and the Kentucky delegates' votes. The presidential candidate and his coterie of friends tried on several occasions early in the new year to solicit Barkley's public sanction.

Finally, in March, Roosevelt's lieutenant, Homer Cummings, offered Barkley the post of temporary chairman and keynote speaker for the Democratic National Convention. Although Barkley eventually intended to endorse Governor Roosevelt, the offer of the prestigious job of keynote speaker, the type of prominent role in national politics that would place Barkley's name in good stead with his constituents, prompted him to make his declaration of support earlier than originally planned. So on March 22, 1932, the Paducah politician publicly endorsed FDR for the presidency of the United States. The arrangement worked out between Barkley and Roosevelt in March seemed crass to some journalists and editors who raised a mercifully brief cry of "corrupt bargain" in the press, but such bargains are the very stuff of politics. Roosevelt received the support he needed and Barkley the prestige he required for the upcoming election campaign.

Thus, over the next several months Barkley struggled many hours and conferred at length with Governor Roosevelt over the text of what proved to be one of the longest and most memorable keynote speeches ever delivered in the history of the national party conclaves. When the Democratic convention opened in Chicago on the warm day of June 27, the audience had already endured an extended session before the strains of "My Old Kentucky Home" brought Barkley to the rostrum and the delegates to their feet. Dressed in an immaculate white suit that would soon betray the effects of movie lights and a sweltering hall, Barkley faced an enthusiastic group which, nonetheless, had had its patience tested by a rambling opening prayer, the singing of two verses of the recently designated national anthem, "The Star-Spangled Banner," welcoming remarks by the Chicago mayor, the reciting in toto of President Thomas Jefferson's Inaugural Address, and a greeting by the retiring chairman of the Democratic National Committee that turned into a full-fledged speech.

When he began his keynote address, Barkley wasted no time; in fact, he hurried his cadence. In addition, for a man famous for humor, his speech turned out to be deadly serious. While he fondly reminded the convention's delegates of the era under President Woodrow Wilson, he severely castigated President Hoover and the previous Republican administrations. As humorist Will Rogers later wrote: "Now comes Senator Barkley with the 'keynote.' What do you mean, 'note'? This is no note. This was in three volumes. . . . But it had to be a long speech for when you start enumerating the things that the Republicans have got away with in the last twelve years you have cut yourself out a job." Barkley's speech was indeed long-winded, but the time he took to deliver his remarks was stretched considerably by interruptions. The greatest interruption came when the prohibitionist keynoter stated: "In order, therefore, to obtain the present will of the American people on this subject of universal controversy, this convention should in the platform here to be adopted recommend the passage by Congress of a resolution repealing the Eighteenth Amendment." The pandemonium that erupted took forty-five minutes to quell. Dances, parades, and fistfights occurred spontaneously while the band played such tunes as "How Dry I

Am." In his enthusiasm to restrain the riot he had caused, Barkley nearly decapitated the rostrum's battery of microphones with his heavy gavel.

Barkley's complete remarks about prohibition were far more sensible than the delegates' reactions. He had never been and never would be a full participant in the "bourbon and burgoo" tradition of Kentucky politics. And the comments he made at the 1932 convention were often misconstrued. The senator did not really advocate prohibition's repeal. He wanted the laws of the land and the Constitution of the United States altered or enforced. Thus he urged the convention to adopt a platform that asked Congress to allow the American people to express unequivocally their feelings about alcoholic beverages. Specifically Barkley suggested that state conventions specially called should decide whether the Eighteenth Amendment should be retained or withdrawn. Subsequently, the American people did have a chance to make the choice and they repealed the Eighteenth Amendment to the Constitution by approving the Twenty-first.

Under different circumstances Barkley's words on prohibition might have choked his political career and sounded the death knell for his reelection in Kentucky. Certainly his dry constituents expressed their deep and at times outraged disappointment to their senator. However, the depression, not prohibition, would be the central campaign issue in the Commonwealth and across the nation. While the Republicans renominated the punctilious and grim Hoover, the Democrats selected the flexible and flamboyant Roosevelt who promised what most Americans desperately wanted, a "New Deal" for their ruined lives. The prestige Barkley acquired as the keynote speaker enabled him to run a diffident but tremendously successful campaign in the party's primary, and the depression handed all Kentucky Democrats running for national office a resounding victory that rivaled that of the Democratic presidential ticket.

The fall campaign's results and Barkley's keynote speech marked a watershed in America's life and Barkley's career.

When, as a prohibitionist, he called for another mandate on the national experiment, Barkley's surprising position reflected the nation's desire to sweep away worn-out and unworkable ideals and solutions that had failed to meet complex problems. In the altered direction the United States would take, Barkley's speech became the opening salvo in what would be described as the New Deal period of American history. Yet in many respects, Barkley was a "New Dealer" long before the term appeared. As a progressive Democrat, he had felt the United States Congress and government ought to assume some responsibility for the people's welfare—a central concept in the New Deal philosophy. This belief had been strengthened in Barkley's mind during this period of transitions and troubled times by his visit to Russia and by his perception of President Hoover's inept response to the depression. Barkley's background, his experience, and his progressive lineage enabled him to assume a major role as a national spokesman and political leader during the dramatic and eventful years of the several Roosevelt administrations.

Barkley and the Senate Committee Investigating Campaign Expenditures interview Governor Al Smith (1928). *Pictured*: Senators Barkley, J. B. Mc-Master, Frederick Steiwer, Sam Bratton, and Governor Al Smith (seated in front)

President Roosevelt stops in Kentucky to speak for the reelection of his "Dear Alben" (1938). *Pictured:* unidentified, Shackleford Miller, Mrs. Cecil Cantrill, FDR, Barkley

Pausing for photographers after a White House Conference with President Roosevelt (1941). *Pictured:* Vice President Henry Wallace, Speaker of the House Sam Rayburn, Senate Majority Leader Barkley, House Majority Leader John W. McCormack

Prime Minister Winston Churchill delivers a message
before a joint session of Congress (December 1941).

Barkley and A. B. "Happy" Chandler push for the sale of war bonds (1942).

After Barkley resigned as Senate majority leader, he reads to the press FDR's letter asking him not to resign (February 1944).

President Harry S. Truman and Barkley at the 1948 convention shortly after their nominations for president and vice president.

The Veep (1951).

5

FRANKLIN'S "DEAR ALBEN"

During the fall election campaign Senator Alben W. Barkley accompanied Governor Franklin D. Roosevelt on a whistle-stop tour of Kentucky. As the train entered each station the polio-stricken presidential nominee moved with assistance to the rear of the train where he joined the senator on the platform for a few brief remarks. When the train rolled into Republican country and entered Corbin, Kentucky, the size of the crowd amazed and thrilled Barkley. Even under normal circumstances he would not simply greet a crowd and introduce the nominee; he forgathered. But the tremendous turnout in the Corbin station inspired Barkley to exhibit his special talents.

"My friends," he began, "it has been four years since I spoke in Corbin, so naturally I cannot call every individual in this great crowd by name. But I can recognize that you are the same people I addressed here four years ago. The reason I know you are the same people is that, after four years of Hoover, you are all wearing the same clothes that you had on four years ago!" The crowd roared its approval for this satirical comment and FDR never forgot the incident. He learned that Barkley's clever anecdotes and avuncular charm overlay the serious purpose he was about.

This magical touch evinced by Barkley, coupled with his

65

progressive philosophy and legislative ability, would make him during the New Deal era a leader for Congress, the Democratic party, and, in particular, the president of the United States. The latter asserted on Inauguration Day, March 4, 1933, "that the only thing we have to fear is fear itself." Added to his confidence-inspiring words was a promise to tackle problems the United States faced with the same spirit, dedication, and sacrifice America had witnessed during the Great War. Those thousands who attended the ceremony plus the millions who huddled about their home radio sets heard the president request from Congress "broad Executive powers to wage a war against the emergency, as great as the power that would be given to me if we were in fact invaded by a foreign foe." The president also felt the country's pulse and stated, "This nation asks for action, and action now."

Barkley and Congress responded to this plea with a massive outpouring of bills that legislated sweeping reforms unparalleled in numbers and scope. The Kentucky senator entered the lists as a knight-errant for the nation's battle against depression. Equally important to his positions in the Finance, Banking and Currency, and Interstate Commerce committees was the role he assumed as assistant to Joseph T. Robinson, Senate majority leader and Barkley's rival for the 1928 vice-presidential nomination. The man from Paducah buttonholed colleagues, debated measures, effected compromises, and secured votes for the host of bills Democrats lovingly and Republicans disparagingly have called FDR's alphabet soup: AAA (Agricultural Adjustment Act), NIRA (National Industrial Recovery Act), FERA (Federal Emergency Relief Act), and many others.

As seen in his remarkable canvass for votes during the 1923 governor's primary, Barkley rarely tired from work or shied away from controversy. He devised few new ideas or directions for administration bills, though he often received some of the most difficult and demanding legislative assignments. For example, when the president decided to use inflation to stimulate the economy and removed the dollar from the gold standard, Robinson handed Barkley the job of guiding the gold-repeal resolution through the Senate. The success he achieved occurred not only through the lopsided majority Democrats enjoyed and the emergency situation Congress confronted but also through Barkley's use of his vast experience, debating skills, solid arguments, and slashing wit that could dismiss as an antiquarian fetish the conservative's love for precious metal.

Increasingly Barkley spoke not only in the Senate chamber but also across the country's airwaves in national radio addresses designed to defend the New Deal. Significantly, the Democratic National Committee selected him in July 1934 to respond on radio to partisan attacks delivered by Henry P. Fletcher, chairman of the Republican party. The position that was thrust on Barkley as national spokesman reflected the rare gathering of all those improbable events in life which, once in a great while, produce the ideal result. So perfect was Barkley in this new dimension that his party turned him into its devastating weapon to confute Republicans in the 1934 congressional elections, when he launched a twenty-state blitzkrieg to defend the New Deal and its candidates.

The very term *New Deal* became more synonymous with Barkley than with any other political figure of the 1930s except Roosevelt himself. In fact the premier student of Barkley as speaker, Raymond Mofield, has claimed that Barkley first coined the phrase which labeled FDR's first two terms in the White House. However, it would be a gross error to confuse Barkley's New Deal identity with his ideology. He had matured politically under President Woodrow Wilson and had assumed Wilson's vision of America as a nation where individual enterprise and competition should not be jeopardized by monopoly capitalism. Certainly the New Deal's shotgun approach hit or employed every possible tactic in the broader strategy to stall and overcome the depression's course. This all-embracing effort could not please everyone, least of all Barkley. The senator felt ill at ease with deficit spending and with the collective thrust of the New Deal, evidenced particularly by the National Recovery Administration (NRA), an agency which encouraged industrywide associations of manufacturers that set prices, standards, and wages for each industry.

This move toward national planning received a sweeping rebuke on "Black Monday," May 27, 1935, when the Supreme Court declared three important pieces of New Deal legislation unconstitutional. Among other casualties, the NRA was struck down. Joined with the perceptible growth of conservative opposition and lower-middle-class disaffection with the New Deal, "Black Monday" shocked and aroused the president into renewed activity. No longer would FDR attempt to mobilize all sectors of society. Instead he chose to scorn wealthy industrialists and financiers whom he described with so much relish as "economic royalists." Hence in June the president called a special session of Congress and unveiled the so-called second New Deal. Social reform, not government planning, became the watchword for FDR, who committed himself to promote the "common man's" interests and the small businesses' survival. In a message to Congress on June 19, the president claimed that without "small enterprises our competitive economic society would cease. Size begets monopoly." Roosevelt, rather than Barkley, built the ideological structure that bridged the chasm between his New Deal and Wilson's New Freedom program that enabled Barkley to move across and align himself so perfectly with FDR's position.

Thus Barkley wholeheartedly gave his voice and energy to promoting those bills President Roosevelt supported as part of his second New Deal: Banking Act, Holding Company Act, Revenue Act, Social Security Act, and the Wagner Labor Relations Act. These measures reinforced a competitive economy, encouraged the labor movement's growth, strengthened federal control over financial institutions, and implemented a social program for unemployment compensation and retirement benefits that allowed the American worker a cushion against life's vicissitudes. The merger of Barkley's usual partisanship with his advocacy for these bills found a significant outlet when the senator acted as majority leader by guiding several of these reforms through Congress's upper house.

In spite of Barkley's keen interest in Roosevelt's program, he retained, as always, a firm line of independence. For years Barkley had sought direct relief for World War veterans. Late in 1935 he and his friends on the Finance Committee wrote a new bonus bill. Disregarding Roosevelt's arguments that the government could ill afford to spend extra funds, Barkley pushed for his long-term commitment to veterans' relief. The president expressed his displeasure with Congress by vetoing the bill on January 20, 1936. Much to FDR's chagrin, Barkley joined with the overwhelming numbers of senators who swept aside the veto and passed the bill a few days later.

Fortunately for Barkley, his crowd of senatorial friends and fellow Democrats who voted with him against the president prevented the Kentucky senator from being singled out for FDR's ire. In fact by 1936, an election year, the shrewd president did not dare speak out against Barkley whose public addresses and radio speeches had made at least his voice a part of the family for millions of households across the nation. Instead of chastising Barkley, President Roosevelt bowed to political reality and selected his normally loyal lieutenant for the historically unique role of delivering the second consecutive keynote address before a national political convention. Administration decisions reached in April made Senate Majority Leader Robinson permanent chairman and his assistant, Barkley, temporary chairman for the Democratic gathering of 1,200 delegates which opened at Philadelphia on Monday, June 22.

The Democratic convention of 1936 differed dramatically from the one held four years earlier. The renomination of Roosevelt was a foregone conclusion. Another difference was the role of the media, particularly the radio, in setting the tone if not the schedule of the convention's proceedings. By 1936 the radio had become a significant fact of domestic and political life. Some twenty-five million sets blanketed the country. For the political conventions three national networks linked two hundred stations for coast-to-coast coverage of what has always been one of the country's favorite spectator pastimes: the selection and election of the American president. Technological improvements allowed dozens of microphones to be dispersed in the hall and stimulated public-conscious delegates who wanted to impress the party's listening constituents. In addition, the Columbia Broadcasting System instituted the first portable pickup to give unprecedented immediacy to the clipping, staccatolike comments of newscaster H. V. Kaltenborn. Also, radio coverage forced convention planners to move the keynote address from Monday afternoon to Tuesday evening at 10:00 P.M. so that an estimated 78 million Americans could hear Barkley's words. Finally, Barkley himself had to restrain his exuberance and keep his remarks within the one hour's broadcast time allotted for his address.

"We are assembled here," spoke Barkley in his opening statement, "not merely to defend but to proclaim the New Deal as the surest highway to that life, liberty, and the pursuit of happiness to which Thomas Jefferson devoted his life." Naturally, Barkley berated Hoover and praised Roosevelt by placing the latter at the end of Barkley's list of great Democrats: Jefferson, Jackson, and Wilson. Considering that everyone present and most of the listeners knew whom the convention would choose as its presidential candidate, Barkley did a remarkable job in maintaining fresh interest for his address. His judicious use of anecdotes and satire and his animated and rousing gesticulations, frequently flailing his fist into his open palm or on the rostrum's lectern, enthralled his viewers. Reflecting on the recently enacted Republican platform, Barkley sent the delegates into spasms of laughter as he stated with an audible snort, flick of his nose, and shrug of his shoulders, "To call this a platform is flattering indeed. It is a revolving eye that looks in all directions and sees nothing."

Although Barkley had no political bombshells to drop as he had four years earlier when he disrupted the convention by his comments on prohibition, he did deliver what has become a classic in the annals of political satire. The convention went wild as Barkley defended AAA practice of reducing crops and livestock to raise farm prices. Republicans, Barkley cleverly stated, "have wept over the slaughter of a few little pigs as if they had been tender human infants nestling at their mothers' breasts. They have shed these tears over the premature death of pigs as if they had been born, educated, and destined for the ministry or for politics. But their bitterest tears are not shed over the fate of little pigs. Their real grief comes from the slaughter of the fat hogs of privilege." A tumultuous demonstration led by convivial Kentucky governor A. B. "Happy" Chandler greeted the end of Barkley's classic, stirring, and partisan keynote address. The speech, so well received by Democrats, proved to be one of the highlights for an otherwise cut-and-dried convention.

Only months later would Barkley realize that within his keynote address lay the seeds of future Democratic discord, nationwide controversy, and a tragic event that, nonetheless, would elevate Barkley to new heights of leadership and responsibility. "Is the court," Barkley asked the delegates, "beyond criticism? May it be regarded as too sacred to be disagreed with?" Barkley spoke, of course, about the Supreme Court whose members, the nine "old men," by their negative decisions threatened to dismantle, piece by piece, the entire New Deal edifice. Certainly, the keynoter had conversed with President Roosevelt about the speech on several occasions in the two months between the announcement of Barkley's appointment as temporary chairman and keynoter and the moment he delivered his remarks. Roosevelt may have expressed to the Kentucky senator his views on the anti-New Deal trend the Supreme Court had taken, but the thoughts Barkley expressed were his own. The senator spurned ghostwriters and had banged his own thoughts out on his weathered typewriter that comfortably adapted itself to Barkley's heavy-handed touch.

Regardless of the initiative Barkley made, it would be the president who would transform the senator's trial balloon into a full-fledged attack on the Supreme Court. Roosevelt rolled into his second term on an avalanche of votes that won him all the electoral votes save those from Maine and Vermont. At this zenith of his power, the president sent to Congress on February 5, 1937, his design for reorganizing the federal judiciary. The plan would permit the president to invigorate the judiciary by appointing a new federal judge for each member of the bench over seventy years of age. If Congress had agreed to this "court-packing" plan, FDR would have had the opportunity to pick as many as six new justices for the Supreme Court alone. Even though Roosevelt and Congress had every constitutional right to implement the proposal, many Americans were aghast by this blatant political effort to give FDR the power to refashion the Supreme Court along pro-New Deal lines. The "reform" threatened to throw the Democratic party in disarray as conservative and southern Democratic senators formed a bloc to oppose Roosevelt. Despite the fact that Robinson, Barkley, and other Roosevelt loyalists had not been consulted before February 5, they fought as hard as they could against growing odds to prevent Democratic ranks from collapsing in face of this controversy.

Then on July 14, 1937, shortly before a vote was to be taken on the court reform bill, Robinson's maid entered her employer's apartment and found the majority leader slumped over dead on the bathroom floor. Nearby lay the *Congressional Record*. Apparently the strain of trying to hold Democrats together on FDR's plan proved too much for Robinson. The fatal heart attack first deferred and then spelled the end of the court-packing measure. When the Senate opened for the day's session, several senators actually spoke in terms of the late majority leader's demise as God's sign of displeasure with FDR's bill. This drivel, which occurred even before the Senate could officially acknowledge the leader's passing, so incensed Barkley that he wrote a note on the matter to Roosevelt.

The president composed his reply the next day while Barkley sat mourning in Hysont's Funeral Parlor. Roosevelt's response expressed his concern for judiciary legislation and sorrow for Robinson's death. But the letter's contents were not nearly so important as the salutation, "Dear Alben," and Roosevelt's pointed reference to Barkley's role as the Senate's acting majority leader. These references startled many anti-New Deal Democrats who rallied around popular and conservative Mississippi Senator Pat Harrison as their choice for Senate leader. It seemed to these men that Roosevelt was acting like a medieval pope in attempting to crown Robinson's successor. Indeed, the president's words alerted liberal senators to line up behind the progressive Barkley for the upcoming vote that would decide who would direct Senate affairs.

The train that carried Robinson's body back to his home in Little Rock, Arkansas, was not really a funeral train. It was a rolling, puffing, rocking political caucus. Sadness aplenty infected the feelings of the thirty-eight senators who accompanied Robinson on his last journey, but everyone on board had on their minds the grandest politics imaginable in the United States Senate. Not since Robinson's election on December 4, 1923, had Democratic senators had the opportunity to pick a leader. Coincidence had little to do with Roosevelt's decision to send as his representatives to the funeral his best lobbyists and congressional liaisons: Postmaster General James Farley, Assistant Attorney General Joseph Keenan, and Undersecretary of the Interior Charles West. Barkley later claimed and contemporary accounts confirm that the man from Paducah made no effort to politick on his own behalf—a style and trait Barkley carried with him at those times when crucial events determined his future. Instead Barkley, like his rival Harrison, remained quietly in his compartment. However, where two or more senators gathered every other nook and cranny of the train became a miniconvention. The constant buzz on the three-day ride to Little Rock and back was only briefly interrupted by the solemn interlude of the funeral.

Shortly after the train returned to Washington's Union Station, seventy-five Democratic senators ambled into the large marble caucus room of the Senate Office Building to pick a new man to guide them. Acting Majority Leader Barkley called the group to order and then, turning the chairmanship over to Senate president pro tempore Key Pittman, took a seat among his colleagues. Pittman appointed tellers and a secretary, and Senator Carter Glass volunteered his well-used Panama hat to hold the ballots. One of the back-bench wags broke the tension of the moment with a joke about secret ballots in a "glass" hat. With these formalities apparently completed, the men came forward by alphabetical order and dropped into the hat a piece of folded white cardboard on which was written the name of their favorite candidate. Suddenly, a thought flashed across the mind of Texas Senator Tom Connally. "Mr. President," Connally spoke in his unmistakable Southwest drawl as he rose to his feet, "we haven't nominated anybody yet. I therefore ask unanimous consent that we consider the Senator from Mississippi, Mr. Harrison, and the Senator from Kentucky, Mr. Barkley, as candidates." After Barkley and Harrison supporters had politicked for days this fine parliamentary point seemed pointedly silly and brought nervous laughter from the excited crowd. Without objection from the floor Pittman so ordered the nominations and one by one the senators again brought their ballots forward until Burton K. Wheeler put the last slip of cardboard into the hat. The tellers then began to read out the names. A tighter race could not be pictured. When seventy-four votes had been counted Barkley and Harrison each had thirty-seven. Barkley later admitted to a *Time* magazine reporter that the final ballot looked as "big as a quilt." The Kentucky senator who dallied with a pipe from time to time bit off its stem as the teller shouted out the last vote, "Barkley!" Amid the resulting tumult, Pat Harrison stepped up and quite graciously moved that the election be made unanimous.

On August 10, 1937, Democratic senators held a victory celebration for Barkley in the Pall Mall Room of Washington's Raleigh Hotel. On top of the head table sat a birdcage containing two fluttering symbols of peace, a pair of doves.

A sizable number of the sixty-six senators attending the dinner had voted against Barkley for the leadership post; yet they all thunderously applauded a tribute to the Kentucky senator delivered by Harrison. President Roosevelt further set the tone for the evening's affair by sending a message that praised Barkley by stating, "He knows by sound instinct that on occasion party harmony is aided and abetted by close harmony." Indeed the only discords for the evening's events appeared when Barkley raised his voice to treat his colleagues to his favorite song, "Wagon Wheels." However, the next day's incidents were more symbolic of Barkley's life in this early period of his new position.

The morning of August 11 began well enough. Barkley gave the Senate's president an agenda that included a vote on one bill and consideration of another, the District of Columbia Airport measure which Senator William H. King was to introduce. The Senate voted on the one bill, but before King could get to his feet New York's Robert Wagner stood up and moved that the Senate proceed to an anti-lynching bill. Thus the new majority leader and King were caught off guard. Regardless of the anti-lynching law's merit this change in the Senate's calendar destroyed Barkley's legislative plans and signaled a filibuster by southern members. In the afternoon Barkley tried his own trick to regain initiative and control over Senate affairs. He moved to adjourn rather than recess the day's session in order to clear the calendar for a new start the following morning. Not only did Democrats split on Barkley's strategy but the wily minority leader, Charles McNary, seeing his opportunity to cause some mischief, countered with a request to recess. As senators entered the Senate's doors for a roll-call vote, Oklahoma's freshman senator, Joshua Lee, asked Barkley how he should vote. "I don't know!" Barkley snapped in despair, "Ask McNary! He's the only real leader around here. That was a hell of a harmony dinner we had last night." McNary's motion carried 36-23.

Barkley's inexperience and the fact that he had to contend with Democratic senators divided along pro- and anti-New

Deal lines made Barkley's first few months miserable and his appeals ineffectual. Also, the failure of Roosevelt's heavy-handed attack on the Supreme Court kindled criticism from the press which declared open season on New Deal programs. As often as not the guns of the press fired point-blank at the New Deal's longtime proponent. The majority leader suffered mental anguish while watching journalists vying with one another in casting cute alliterations, such as "bumbling Barkley," to describe the Kentucky senator.

If these aspersions were not enough, Barkley's philosophy on party unity and the majority leader's role laid him wide open to the final insult the wretched label "party hack" that stuck to him like glue to wood and still colors descriptions of Barkley's character. Most Americans do not realize that the majority leader in House or Senate is not a constitutional position but one that evolved in the twentieth century. Specifically, the position of Senate majority leader became an institution during the Progressive Era and received final definition during the administration of Barkley's political mentor, President Wilson. As political scientist Randall Ripley has noted, when the president belongs to the same party as the majority leader, the leader's job is to organize the chamber along party lines, schedule bills, promote attendance, distribute and collect information, and persuade members. The leader does not initiate legislation or criticize the president, but rather acts as the president's alter ego in Congress. Barkley's counterpart in the House, Congressman Joseph Byrns of Tennessee, once told the press, "I have no statement about legislative plans, except I expect to put through the plans and policies of President Roosevelt." And Robinson had expressed the same sentiment at the conclusion of the Seventy-third Congress in June 1934, "Under the leadership of President Roosevelt this Congress has done a wonderful work."

Barkley met with Roosevelt every Monday for a conference in the Oval Office in the Executive wing of the White House. The senator and other Democratic leaders discussed legislative matters and priorities with the convivial, charismatic, and powerful president. No one, including Barkley, felt restrained from expressing their thoughts, but once the leaders left the conference they spoke as one in public on the measures discussed *in camera*. The respect Barkley held for party unity, his historically proved progressivism, his conception of the majority leader's role as fashioned under his hero Wilson and refined by his esteemed predecessor combined to make Barkley appear a simple-minded sycophant for President Roosevelt. It was much easier for the press to call the majority leader a "party hack" than to investigate the complicated pattern of past experiences that led Barkley to support the president so strongly on all key issues.

One notable Kentucky figure perceived these public criticisms and evident weaknesses that afflicted Barkley as an opportunity for political advancement. The relatively youthful, thirty-nine-year-old governor, Albert Benjamin "Happy" Chandler capped Barkley's problems by challenging the newly elected Senate majority leader for his seat in the 1938 Democratic primary. Ever since Chandler had won the post of lieutenant governor in 1931, his political star had risen brightly, based on his popular programs, good looks, smooth tenor voice, dynamolike energy, and a grin *Baltimore Evening Sun* correspondent Henry Hyde called, "one of the widest and most captivating in the political arena." Ironically, Chandler considered himself a "New Dealer," had received Barkley's endorsement for the governor's office, and possessed, like Barkley, a full measure of ambition for national office.

This ambition and the dead-end nature of the governor's term propelled Chandler into an anti-Barkley campaign. He revealed his future course when he declined an invitation to attend a testimonial dinner given in Barkley's honor on January 22, 1938, by Louisville Democrats in the Brown Hotel. The fact that Chandler's absence indicated he would fight Barkley for the nomination bothered Roosevelt. He sent to Louisville some of the heaviest guns in his political arsenal to let Kentuckians know that the president wanted them to reelect his Senate majority leader. The emissaries included

Roosevelt's personal secretary, Marvin McIntyre, and five senators including Missouri's Harry Truman and Indiana's Sherman Minton. While Barkley and 1,300 guests feasted on boned breast of squab, they listened to McIntyre read a letter from President Roosevelt. "Senator Barkley's long familiarity with national affairs, his integrity, his patriotic zeal, his courage and loyalty, and his eloquence . . . give him exceptional equipment as a legislator and a leader." The warmth of Roosevelt's kind words of praise struck deep in Barkley's heart. The senator was visibly shaken when he responded, "I'd rather deserve a letter like that than hold any office in the land."

An entirely different set of emotions appeared at a luncheon held at Louisville's Pendennis Club and a dinner the following Saturday at the Seelbach Hotel. Chandler and his friends planned these rival functions to detract from the honors Barkley received and to illustrate the power Chandler possessed. The governor obliquely announced his candidacy: "If by chance you people want me to represent you in any other capacity . . . I won't call upon any senators or any other fellows from the North to come help me." These remarks became the essence of Chandler's platform.

Between the January dinners and the August primary, Chandler continued to attack Barkley as an outsider. In the governor's opinion, the senator had spent so much time away from home that somehow he had lost his Kentucky heritage and had to use "northerners" to help him gain votes. Chandler rarely referred to the senator by name but he employed the sobriquet "Old Alben" for the sixty-year-old Barkley in order to assert identity with younger constituents. Following the lead of national news commentators, the governor also picked up the beat to drum into voters "bumbling Barkley's" reputation as an administration "yes-man" who had stopped trying to legislate the Commonwealth's fair share of federal funds. The governor also reminded Kentucky audiences that Barkley's daughters married and lived beyond the Commonwealth's borders: Marian had wed Washington attorney Max O'Rell Truitt while Laura Louise traveled the world with her husband, Douglas MacArthur II, a foreign service officer and nephew of the famed general. Chandler failed to mention David Barkley's career in the United States Army Air Force and the Bureau of Air Commerce and the purchase by Alben and Dorothy the previous year of Angles, a rambling, single-storied, pre-Civil War brick home near Paducah that housed three decades of mementos Barkley collected in his years of public service to McCracken County and Kentucky citizens.

As on previous occasions, Barkley converted alleged weaknesses into strengths. The durable senator dismissed out of hand the "Old Alben" tag by assailing the voters with his vigorous speeches eight to fifteen times in a single day's canvass. As for his cosmopolitan family, Barkley possessed what only a father could, pride in his offspring's accomplishments. But most of all the senator stood foursquare behind the New Deal. Kentucky farmers, workers, and businessmen had received equal benefits with their counterparts across the country from the national effort to soften and reduce the depression's effects. The more Chandler probed into New Deal themes the easier it became for Barkley to question the governor's liberal sympathies.

This unfolding pattern of Chandler's New Deal position drew national attention, but Kentucky's 1938 senatorial primary also gained considerable play in the national press for two other reasons. First, the charges of corruption exchanged by both camps fed titillating story after story for articles that exposed the backwoods, backslapping, and backstairs nature peculiar to some Kentucky elections. Later studies of this primary have generally exonerated Barkley and Chandler from questionable practices. Nevertheless, contemporary accounts indicate there is little doubt that Barkley's overly anxious friends used federal programs to grease the axles of the senator's political bandwagon while Chandler's men employed the machinery of state government to boost the governor's campaign. Second, Roosevelt brought nationwide notoriety to the Barkley-Chandler battle by his consistent interest in the reelection of his majority leader.

Roosevelt set a trend for future chief executives by devising a southern strategy—to plug for political friends or weed out political enemies particularly in the South so as to break the congressional bloc of conservative Democrats that delayed or stymied New Deal legislation. The president placed Barkley's renomination and election at the base of the southern strategy. Should Barkley lose, the president's aspirations for the future would be dashed irreparably in the Senate and his designs for a renovated Congress crushed against the rocks of conservative opposition. Thus it was Roosevelt who not only sent his top campaigners into the Bluegrass State but also took the unusual step on July 8, 1938, of a personal visit. Publicly FDR denied any meddling in Kentucky politics, and in fact Chandler joined Barkley on the platform for the principal speech Roosevelt delivered before an audience at Covington's Latonia Race Track. "But," Roosevelt said as he referred to Chandler, "I think he would be the first to acknowledge that as a very junior member of the Senate it would take him many, many years to match the national knowledge, the experience and the acknowledged leadership in the affairs of our nation of that son of Kentucky of whom the whole nation is proud—Alben Barkley."

Shortly before the primary Chandler claimed to have been made ill from water fouled by a Barkley supporter and was forced to stop campaigning a week before the August election. The incident might have caused a sympathy vote for the governor but Barkley once again turned damaging circumstances to his advantage. "My managers," Barkley later remarked, "gravely announced the addition of an 'ice water guard,' also a 'food taster,' to my staff. Every time someone would pour me a glass of water at a speaking engagement, I would hold it up and look quizzically at the crowd. With obvious delight the people would take their cue and yell, 'Careful! It may be poisoned!' I would shudder fearfully and put it down." Hence the skillful politician defeated Chandler by over 70,000 votes and went on to gain reelection for the second time by overwhelming his Republican opponent, Louisville Judge John P. Haswell, who received a scant 38 percent of the vote.

Barkley's victory highlighted the otherwise dim election returns for 1938 that showed President Roosevelt had failed miserably in his initiative to mold Congress to his views. Indeed, the president was fortunate to retain the services of such an able and loyal legislator. It took, for example, every ounce of Barkley's knowledge and charm merely to fund a deficiency appropriation for the Works Progress Administration (WPA) in the 1939 congressional session and then for only a fraction of the administration's original request. The compromise Barkley effected to secure some monies for the New Deal's principal federal relief program did little to endear him to FDR, and Barkley's position—something is better than nothing—disclosed he had at times to be influential in Congress in order to promote or, in the case of the WPA, to salvage the administration's broader goals.

Nevertheless, Barkley's successes far outweighed his failures and drew for him the respect he had not received when first selected to lead the Senate. Even Washington's sensitive and critical press corps began to note the rise in Barkley's expertise and power. After a difficult and lengthy fight Congress amended the Hatch Act in 1940 by extending the reform to prohibit federally funded state employees from engaging in politics. The *Washington Daily News* minced no words in proclaiming that the revised Hatch Act represented a "monument to Alben Barkley's persistence and parliamentary skill." Barkley could not shake loose from all his detractors. But increasingly these critics could be isolated and identified as strident partisans such as Joseph Alsop and Robert Kintner who wrote by-line articles for the Republican-oriented *Saturday Evening Post* and anonymous stories for the conservative weekly *Time* magazine.

The improved position Barkley had earned and the national reputation he had already acquired forced Roosevelt to confide to Barkley shortly before the 1940 Democratic convention, "You know, some folks here at the White House are for you for the Democratic nomination as my successor." However, the president was about to spurn tradition and seek a third term. FDR's earlier concern to strengthen his congressional hand for domestic reasons had been overshadowed by foreign events. On September 1, 1939, Hitler had sent Germany's armies storming into Poland, initiating events that would lead to a second World War. The United States retained a precarious neutrality, but by the time the Democratic convention opened in Chicago in mid-July the Western world's great democracies, save England, had fallen as Germany, Italy, and Japan built a fascist world order based on conquest that disturbed and distressed more Americans with each passing day.

The president, fearful of abandoning the nation's helm while the ship of state steamed into stormy waters not only decided to seek a third term but also to drop his older and conservative vice president, John Nance Garner, in favor of the younger and liberal Henry A. Wallace, the controversial secretary of agriculture. FDR's choice of Wallace did not please Barkley who said as much to the chief executive when the two met for one of their Monday conferences. There is enough evidence from Barkley's tortuous private and public statements about the qualifications of Wallace to infer that Barkley wanted the vice presidency for himself. The self-effacing senator did not test his relationship with Roosevelt by pushing forward his name as an alternative. In Roosevelt's judgment in June 1940, Barkley's mastery over legislative procedures and Senate affairs undoubtedly eliminated him from consideration for the second place on the ticket. If elected for a third term, Roosevelt would need Barkley's strong and faithful support in Congress.

Barkley was one of only a handful of presidential advisers who knew the direction of FDR's thoughts before the Democrats met in Chicago for their convention. The president moved cautiously over the third-term issue. Although he remained extremely popular with rank-and-file Democrats, Roosevelt's violation of American tradition raised by the possibility of his nomination and election in 1940 stuck like underchewed food in the throats of many Democratic leaders, including several of FDR's longtime associates. The safest course the president could travel was to be drafted by the delegates in a popular acclamation, which would neutralize the Republican charge that Roosevelt merely possessed an insatiable appetite for power. In these delicate matters, Barkley walked deftly, if not obligingly, as the chief executive's stalking-horse.

Honored by his selection as the convention's permanent chairman, Barkley presented an address early in the evening of July 16. His remarks followed those delivered the previous day by James Farley, chairman of the Democratic National Committee, and Convention Keynoter William B. Bankhead. The latter two speakers had studiously avoided mentioning Roosevelt's name. With spirit and wit Barkley lauded the administration's domestic and foreign policies and excoriated Republicans whose earlier convention had produced a platform written, so Barkley claimed, "in mud by the migratory feet of a weasel." The electrifying moment came, however, when Barkley concluded, "And now, my friends, I have an additional statement to make in behalf of the President of the United States." Barkley's proclamation sparked the audience and signaled the start of a wild demonstration as gallery spectators left their seats and joined delegates in chanting, "We Want Roosevelt." When a semblance of order had been reestablished twenty minutes later, Barkley told the conventioneers that the president "wishes in all earnestness and sincerity to make it clear that all the delegates to this convention are free to vote for any candidate." To the delegates, at least, it was clear that "any candidate" also meant Roosevelt. The next day the convention nominated the president on the first ballot. Roosevelt went on to defeat his Republican opponent, Wendell L. Willkie, in the fall election by the convincing margin of 449 to 82 in the electoral college.

The approach and outbreak of war shaped Roosevelt's third term of office and Barkley's position within that administration. Unlike World War I when America slipped into conflict after a series of mounting crises, World War II came crashing in for the United States when Japanese bombs fell on Pearl Harbor, December 7, 1941. Although his interests lay preeminently with domestic affairs, the Senate majority leader took command over several congressional measures that influenced the direction of America's war efforts and the peace that followed. Even before December 7, Barkley sponsored the Senate's version of the Lend-Lease Act which made billions of dollars available to America's allies. On his own initiative Barkley cemented the warm relations between Great Britain and the United States by inviting British Prime Minister Winston Churchill to speak on December 26, 1941, before a joint session of Congress. The Kentuckian also lobbied consistently for a Jewish homeland in Palestine and introduced a resolution in the spring of 1943 which paved the way for international cooperation in punishing Nazis for their nightmarish persecution of Jews. Finally, Barkley revived Wilson's concept of a League of Nations when he helped draft the Connally-Fulbright Resolution of November 1943 that marked Senate approval for an international organization to maintain peace after the war's conclusion.

Quite naturally Barkley and other legislative leaders assumed a lesser role in external affairs which devolved constitutionally to the United States president. However, and by necessity, Roosevelt's focus on prosecuting the war and maintaining close relations with such diverse allies as Great Britain and Soviet Russia left to Barkley extraordinary powers and interest over domestic issues. With equanimity and aplomb Barkley used his charm, good humor, and ability to compromise in order to pass legislation America needed to win the war. He met regularly with committee heads and hence formed a legislative cabinet to facilitate passage of bills such as the War Powers Acts, which permitted Roosevelt to harness the nation's energy for the worldwide struggle against fascism. Mindful that the home front's high morale influenced America's fighting forces,

Barkley assisted in the passage of a Price Control Act and co-sponsored an Anti-Inflation bill. And ever the liberal even when wartime conditions tended to reduce American freedoms, the majority leader tried unsuccessfully to push through an anti-poll tax bill that would have helped enfranchise southern blacks and poor whites.

Normally Barkley cooperated closely and warmly with President Roosevelt, but the senator's concentration on domestic affairs inevitably led him into conflict with the administration. Unlike the president, Barkley had to live on a day-to-day basis with the varied needs and personalities of congressional colleagues. He also felt compelled to preserve those interests of the American people that Roosevelt neglected because his thoughts converged on foreign matters. Thus, at times, Barkley slid perceptively though almost unconsciously between roles as the administration's tool and watchdog. He did not hesitate, for example, to criticize the War Production Board for its habit of assigning war-related contracts to large rather than small businesses. But the most notorious clash between Barkley and Roosevelt occurred in February 1944 when the senator engineered a stinging rebuke to the president's power.

On February 21 Barkley, Vice President Wallace, House Majority Leader John W. McCormack, and Speaker Sam Rayburn met with Roosevelt in the White House in their regular Monday morning legislative conference. The meeting, though, proved to be most unusual. First, Roosevelt summoned the men to his high-ceilinged bedroom where he conversed with them from his mahogany bed. Second, he announced offhandedly that he intended to do what no other president had dared to do in the nation's history—veto a tax bill. The shock of Roosevelt's words prompted an outcry of protest from Barkley, Rayburn, and McCormack. Earlier, Roosevelt had requested Congress to pass a bill for additional taxes in excess of $10 billion. The Democratic leaders had worked hard to secure legislation, though for only $2.3 billion. Barkley admitted the bill's imperfection to FDR, but the Senate's leader, who also belonged to the Finance Committee, knew that the Senate had done its best. In the bluntest terms, Barkley advised the president to sign the legislation or forfeit all chance to secure any additional funds.

Roosevelt's response to Barkley's advice was received the next day by the House of Representatives in the form of a veto message. The president's move enraged Barkley. He had faithfully served the president who now appeared to take him for granted. Worst of all in Barkley's opinion, Roosevelt had ignored his counsel and had listened to those White House advisers who possessed limited knowledge of the intricate procedures required to pass a tax bill. Tuesday evening when Barkley arrived home, Dorothy agreed that her husband had to lift his voice in protest. About 11:00 P.M., Barkley entered the bedroom with the intention of jotting some notes and typing a few pages of a speech. His mind, though, whirled with emotion and he gave up in frustration. At his office the next morning, however, the words tumbled out so fast that Loraine Winfrey, Barkley's secretary, could barely keep up with the senator's dictation and later completed typing only a half-dozen pages before Barkley had to rush for his front-row seat on the Senate floor.

When Barkley entered the chamber, every eye fell on him. The rumor of his break with the president had spread through Washington, resulting in a packed press gallery. A page brought Barkley a wooden lectern and then in a whisper the majority leader requested his neighbor in the Senate, Kenneth McKellar of Tennessee, to bring to the lectern the remaining portions of the speech. With these preliminaries completed, Barkley put on his glasses, raised his portly frame—draped in an impeccable brown suit—to its full height of nearly six feet, and asked for the floor. The speech he delivered would win him no honors for style and delivery; his voice cracked on several occasions and he stumbled over words. Nevertheless, the circumstances converted Barkley's performance into the most sensational event the Senate had experienced in living memory. Line by line Barkley destroyed the arguments found in Roosevelt's veto message. He saved the most venom for the president's flip phrase: "It is not a tax bill but a tax-relief bill, providing relief not for the needy but for the greedy."

"That statement," Barkley shouted, ". . . is a calculated and deliberate assault upon the legislative integrity of every member of the Congress of the United States. The Congress may do as they please. But as for me, I do not propose to take this unjustifiable assault lying down." Not only did Barkley state that he would tender his resignation as majority leader the next morning, but he urged his associates to override Roosevelt's veto. When Barkley finished, the galleries and Senate floor alike exploded with cheers and applause. While senators from both parties formed lines to shake Barkley's hand, Roosevelt, resting in his Hyde Park library, received the disturbing news of Barkley's attack. Apparently the tenor of Barkley's speech genuinely surprised the president, but not enough for him to lose his manipulative talents. He sent the Kentuckian another famous "Dear Alben" message in time for presidential assistant Stephen Early to deliver it to Barkley (and adroitly to the press) when he arrived home.

"I regret to learn from your speech in the Senate on the tax veto that you thought I had in my message attacked the integrity of yourself and other members of Congress. Such was not my intention," Roosevelt demurred. ". . . I sincerely hope that you will not persist in your announced intention to resign as Majority Leader of the Senate. If you do, however, I hope your colleagues will . . . immediately and unanimously re-elect you." Roosevelt, of course, merely tried to jump in front and lead the parade after he missed its departure. The following morning, as promised, Barkley handed in his resignation to his colleagues and then left the Senate Democratic Conference Room. In a few minutes Senator Connally bolted from the room and cried, "Make way for liberty!" Connally had been delegated to inform Barkley that Senate Democrats had accepted the resignation and then, in the president's words, "immediately and unanimously" reelected him their majority leader.

The "Barkley incident" affected profoundly contemporary events as well as the senator's life, and the repercussions may be with us today. In the immediate context, Barkley's speech spurred House and Senate to override Roosevelt's veto. The senator also discovered that his stature had jumped immeasurably. Even the Republican-controlled press no longer felt obliged to tack "party hack" or "bumbling" beside his name. Naturally, Barkley's relationship with Roosevelt altered noticeably. In the frankest terms, the senator held power as the popularly chosen leader of the Senate and was not beholden to the president. The whole affair established a precedent for independence not found among earlier majority leaders. Finally, his speech kept Barkley from fulfilling his life's ambition, for he might have been president of the United States after April 12, 1945, the date FDR died. In 1944 Roosevelt changed vice presidents again, this time picking Harry S. Truman to be his running mate. Every commentator on this period admits that Barkley, because of the February speech, lost the strong possibility of having his name, rather than Truman's, in the second spot on the Democratic ballot.

Even though Barkley wrote a lengthy article, "Why I Support Roosevelt," for *Collier's* and nominated FDR at the summer Democratic convention, an undercurrent of reserve remained in their relationship. The pair had a reconciliation of sorts after each had won a fourth term in their respective offices and after the president had returned from his Yalta conference. Nevertheless, Roosevelt never brought up the topic of the senator's famous speech and Barkley never offered to apologize for his actions. In many respects, FDR's death dispelled a shadow that hovered over Barkley. Contemporaries finally realized that the Kentuckian possessed the deepest respect for the Congress, his political associates, and the give-and-take of the democratic process— traits sometimes missing from Roosevelt's character. The seemingly indestructible Barkley would endure after FDR's death as the statesman of American politics and Mr. Democrat for his party.

6

A SINGULAR VEEP

FAMED AS A RACONTEUR, Alben W. Barkley kept an audience in stitches by delivering his "Advice to Newly Elected Senators" before the National Press Club on April 4, 1945. He cautioned recently installed senators to run "for the tall and uncut" if they received a letter from the White House that greeted them with the salutation "Dear" followed by their first name. Barkley continued: "I never like to become irritated at the President, but the other day he provoked me to anger. He wrote a letter to Senator Thomas of Utah and addressed him 'Dear Elbert.' Now, think of that. Dear Elbert. I have a patent on this 'dear' business and my patent has not expired, and it will not expire until the President leaves the White House and I leave the Senate, which means that I have a patent in perpetuity on this form of address."

Barkley's remarks, in his specific reference to the president and in his general congenial manner, held an unintentional irony. The nature of man's mortality altered his "in perpetuity" to a fleeting moment—the president died scarcely more than a week later. Also, the humor Barkley displayed in this period before numerous groups had a purpose that bore little resemblance to his political ambitions or legislative concerns. He grabbed every speaking engagement available, and for pay, because he desperately needed money. Ever since Dorothy's failing health revealed a debilitating heart disease, she required constant medical attention and nursing care that made the couple's last few years together a financial nightmare. Alben and Dorothy sold their Washington home and moved to an apartment. Convenience and necessity forced a nostalgic return to the way of life they shared in their early years in the nation's capital.

Only a handful of intimate friends knew the double burden Alben carried until Dorothy's death on March 10, 1947. One of these friends, Marny Clifford, wife of President Harry Truman's top adviser Clark, chose her own label for Barkley. "Sparkle Barkle" mirrored the loving mission Barkley undertook with happy grace and apparent ease. In Dorothy's last few years, Alben kept a rigorous pace; during the day he attended to Senate business, and during the evenings or on the weekends he dashed for trains or planes that took him to the speaking engagements he used to earn needed extra money. The touching dedication and comfort he provided Dorothy did not detract from the vital service he performed for his country in the hectic period following the death of President Roosevelt.

The new president found himself in an office he did not expect and assumed an overly humble regard for his ability to fulfill a job fate had thrust upon him. It took a half-joking but stern rebuke from Barkley to get the former Missouri senator to stop calling the majority leader "Boss." After a rocky period, Truman grew into the presidency and exhibited the strong leadership capabilities he possessed. Nevertheless, Truman continued Roosevelt's practice of the Monday morning legislative conferences, and, in the opinion of Truman's last secretary of state, Dean Acheson, Barkley became the administration's "field commander." And Americans required all the best "generals" she could muster.

World War II's conclusion in Europe and Asia in the spring and summer of 1945 left in its wake as many problems as those solved by the Allied victory over Italy, Germany, and Japan. Not the least of these issues concerned the anger Americans retained over the debacle at Pearl Harbor. Barkley sponsored a resolution that called for a House-Senate committee to investigate and answer the disturbing question of why the United States government and military appeared woefully unprepared for Japan's surprise attack. His resolution unanimously passed the Senate on September 6, 1945, and received House approval a few days later. It swept its sponsor into the chairmanship, as Barkley led the ten-member "Joint Committee on the Investigation of the Pearl Harbor Attack." After holding seventy sessions, hearing forty-four witnesses, and gathering 20,000 pages of testimony and evidence, Barkley and the committee rendered its final report on July 20, 1946. Their findings canceled conservatives' indictment that Roosevelt somehow had caused the tragedy. Their imposing effort also brought to light valuable pieces of information about the infamous Pearl Harbor attack that might otherwise have been lost to the nation's history. Finally, the committee exposed the weaknesses in communications among the armed services. This deficiency would later be eliminated by the establishment of a Department of Defense that could coordinate more effectively America's military needs.

Although Barkley devoted nearly a year to this Pearl Harbor project, he continued to function expertly as the majority leader or, after the 1946 elections brought about Republican control of the Senate, minority leader. The killing pace he kept would have undermined the health of a less robust man three decades his junior. In the other innumerable problems he confronted, the Kentuckian's sociable humor perfectly complemented the administration's generally successful bipartisan approach in foreign affairs that found the Senate approving America's entrance into the United Nations, a multibillion-dollar loan to rebuild England's war-ravaged economy, and support for Truman in his dealing with Russian intractability and the containment of communism in Eastern Europe through the so-called Truman Doctrine and Marshall Plan. This bipartisan spirit did not stop Barkley from using hyperbole when he criticized Republicans, but he always avoided personal attacks and his amiable anecdotes and harmless barbs actually helped him form affectionate alliances with many Republicans. His colleagues on both sides of the aisle could trust Barkley to put national interests above parochial concerns.

Republican leader Robert A. Taft was not afraid to compliment Barkley for his strikingly productive and effective work. In fact a poll conducted by *Pageant* magazine among members of Congress placed Barkley and Taft at the head of a list of the hardest-working individuals in the United States Senate. The reputation and popularity Barkley enjoyed were not confined to Congress. He ranked ahead of President Truman as the man most requested of the Democratic Speakers' Bureau. *Look* magazine's roll of fascinating Americans listed Barkley second only to war hero and future president General Dwight D. Eisenhower. And in May 1948 the coveted Collier Award honored Barkley for his distinguished congressional service. The $10,000 prize associated with the award went in Barkley's name to the University of Louisville Medical School. These awards and honors and the esteem with which Barkley was held by Americans in and out of politics go a long way to explain the fortuitous events that surrounded Barkley's life in 1948.

While the year would end on a happy note, it had for Barkley and the Democrats in general a very sour start. Bipartisan cooperation in foreign affairs did not extend to perplexing domestic problems. The conversion of America from wartime to peacetime economies traversed a potholed road that jolted the economy. Pent-up savings were unleashed at the war's end and caused rampant inflation compounded by the paralyzing railroad strike of 1946. These difficulties helped resurrect the Republican party which began to ask Americans, "Had enough?" or proclaim, "To err is Truman." Republicans carried both houses of Congress in 1946 as well as a majority of state administrations. The election appeared to be such a repudiation of Truman that disaffection with the president spread to Democrats, with at least one, Senator J. William Fulbright of Arkansas, publicly calling for Truman's resignation.

The surge away from Democrats in 1946 had a tremendous impact on Congress in 1947 and 1948. Apparently Americans had tired of reformist crusades, and the slide toward conservatism allowed Republicans to throw damaging punches at New Deal ideas. Congress delivered a posthumous, stinging blow to Roosevelt by passing in 1947 the Constitution's Twenty-second Amendment which restricted future presidents to two terms in office. In the same year and over Truman's veto Republicans and their fellow travelers on the Democratic side of the aisle checked and reversed through the Taft-Hartley Act the progress labor had made under FDR. The bill legalized government injunctions in labor disputes and permitted, with state law, open shops to dilute union strength. Barkley did not twitch an inch in the general drift to the right. He sternly condemned the Taft-Hartley bill, and for sound constitutional reasons. If state laws restricted union membership, Barkley argued, "We might as well pass an act of Congress against counterfeiting the currency of the United States, but in it provide that if any State legislature authorizes counterfeiting then the Federal law shall be null and void in the State." After his colleagues failed to heed his arguments, the Kentuckian could be seen from time to time sauntering through the Capitol Building wearing a red, blue, and yellow tie that stated for all who could read it, "Repeal Taft-Hartley Act."

Early in 1948, an election year, President Truman fought back to gain the initiative he had lost over domestic affairs. He began to swamp the Republican Congress with bill after bill that reaffirmed his ties with liberalism. While many a critic advanced the theory that Truman merely spruced up a composite of New Deal ideas, his emphasis on civil rights engraved his unique emblem on those programs that would later be called the Fair Deal. In raising the issue of civil rights, however, the president tied a nearly fatal noose around his neck. Many southern Democrats found it difficult if not impossible to find any sympathy for a dramatic change in the South's social structure. The trends Truman established left the Democratic National Committee no choice but to pick for party spokesman at the forthcoming convention the one man they knew held impeccable liberal credentials and commanded popular support from all factions within the party. Barkley, though, was not so sure he ought to fulfill the unprecedented role of keynote speaker for the third time. When Truman caught wind of Barkley's reluctance, the president insisted and Barkley agreed to deliver the address.

In a mental state of gloom, 1,500 delegates converged on Philadelphia for the ceremonies that opened the Thirtieth Democratic National Convention on Monday, July 12. Many of the delegates and most of the 13,000 plus spectators assumed the Republicans had chosen the next American president, New York Governor Thomas E. Dewey, in the very same Convention Hall three weeks earlier. The threat Dixiecrats carried out later of splintering the party over a civil rights plank, Truman's lackluster appeal, and the apparent end to excitement for New Deal liberalism combined to convince most Democrats that 1948 was a Republican year and the convention an embarrassing formality to be conducted and forgotten as quickly as possible while holding onto hope for 1952. The *New York Times* reported that when workers for the president "gave out Truman Victory kits with whistles, the delegates were so blue and downcast they just put them in their pockets instead of blowing them." In this atmosphere of discouragement Senator J. Howard McGrath, permanent chairman, introduced the keynoter for what was billed as the first day's principal event.

Barkley skipped most of the usual obligatory pleasantries and immediately zeroed in on the theme of his address. "We have," he stated, "a solemn commission from millions of American men and women. We are here to give them an accounting of our stewardship for 16 eventful years, for not one of which we make apology. . . . Our claim upon the confidence of the people rests upon an unparalleled record of devotion to the people's welfare; a record which rescued the American economy of free enterprise from a collapse we did not foster; a record which four times the American people have overwhelmingly endorsed." These stirring words reminded the delegates that they need not consider their New Deal record a liability, but a course of action for which they could be proud. Barkley's sweeping, gesticulating, pounding, formidable presence on the rostrum defied the odds and brought the convention to life.

The orator had never been better. He went on to list New Deal accomplishments: soil conservation, rural electrification, flood control, Labor Relations Act, Fair Labor Standards Act, reciprocal trade, Federal Deposit Insurance Corporation, Federal Housing Administration, Home Owners' Loan Corporation, Commodity Credit Corporation, Export-Import Bank, Securities and Exchange Commission. With each program mentioned the applause grew louder and the interruptions lasted longer until every sentence Barkley delivered threatened to cause a disrupting demonstration. "Let us ask, and let the American people ask," Barkley demanded in his commanding baritone voice, "those who spray this forest of superb accomplishments with the froth of their vindictive lips, which tree will they cut down with their mighty axe or their puny hatchet? In 1947 the Republican party secured control of both branches of the Congress. . . . What has been its record?" By the time Barkley finished the answer to his own question, the Eightieth Congress's "do-nothing" reputation, justifiably or not, had been firmly established.

Truman acknowledged Barkley's rousing performance by tapping him for his running mate. Actually, the president would have preferred Supreme Court Associate Justice William O. Douglas. The man from Missouri understood that picking a fellow border-state politician did not seem to be politically astute. Nevertheless, "The Convention," in the words of James Farley, "made up the President's mind for him." Barkley was not very thrilled to be Truman's second or third choice. He complained that he had been offered a hot biscuit after it had been handed around long enough to get cold. The Kentuckian, though, had to be pleased that the party delegates voted him by acclamation as their nominee. In fact, contemporary accounts clearly indicate that if he had not possessed such reticence and such reverence over the nation's executive offices, he might have challenged Truman with some hope of success for either nomination.

Despite the shaky start in the relationship between the Democratic nominees, their sheer pugnacity, bounding energy, and fighting oratory wedded Barkley and Truman into a truly dynamic team that produced one of the more exciting campaigns witnessed in American history. "I'm going to fight hard," Truman told Barkley, "I'm going to give them hell." The president adopted Barkley's tack of avoiding the names of Republican nominees and instead concentrated his attention on the Republican Congress. And he took a gamble that struck pure gold. During his acceptance speech Truman stated he was calling Congress for a special session to begin on Missouri's "Turnip Day," July 26. The president challenged the Republicans to enact their platform. However, after so many years out of power, GOP politicians were immured in a philosophy of opposition and were unable to move constructively to pass a single piece of significant legislation. Thus Truman nailed down the lid on the coffin Barkley built in his keynote speech that snugly wrapped the Eightieth Congress in a "do-nothing" reputation.

While Republicans marked time in the special session, Barkley worked feverishly with the Democratic National Committee to lay plans for the forthcoming campaign. Committee members assumed erroneously that the septuagenarian would have to conduct a leisurely canvass so as not to overtax his health. The committee originally thought Barkley ought to mimic the style Truman would use of traveling by train in the traditional whistle-stop fashion. However, the vice-presidential nominee had a different idea. He proposed, and the committee finally agreed, to meet his speaking engagements by airplane and hence initiate the first "prop-stop" campaign in national politics. The Democrats rented for Barkley a United Airlines' DC-3, remodeled with a bunk and named "The Bluegrass." This flying headquarters would also carry secretaries, journalists, political advisers, and writers.

After a sojourn in Europe to attend the Interparliamentary Union which met in Rome, Barkley returned to Washington on September 16 for a flurry of last-minute conferences before Truman entrained and Barkley enplaned for the uphill battle to win the election. Shortly before the pair went off on their separate trails, Barkley remarked to Truman, "It's a victorious trip." The confidence these men exuded belied the public opinion polls which predicted a Republican victory. Between Barkley's first stop at Wilkes-Barre, Pennsylvania, on September 18 and his last in Paducah on November 1, the vice-presidential nominee flew to thirty-six states, delivered 250 speeches, and journeyed 150,000 miles. His awesome display of vocal and physical powers reminded journalists that the Iron Man had not become rusty.

In most of the speeches, a blend of prepared and extemporaneous remarks, Barkley played variations on the theme of Democratic successes and Republican failures. He and his assistants, though, made a serious effort to tailor each talk to the crowd in attendance. This personal touch kept the DC-3 just as noisy on the inside with typewriters clacking and mimeographs tumbling as the roaring twin engines did on the outside. Barkley quipped to one reporter midway through the campaign, "I'm a high-altitude thinker." Throughout the strenuous journey Barkley maintained his sense of humor and liberally shared it with his companions and the audiences that met him. A rain-soaked crowd at Dover, Delaware, heard the nominee promise he would reduce the length of his speech. "I don't want," Barkley continued, "you to get your feet wet. In fact, I don't even want you to get 'dewey.' " This oblique reference to the Republican presidential candidate was the exception that proved the rule as Barkley avoided mentioning the opposition by name.

While Barkley and Truman crisscrossed the country, the Republicans maintained banker's hours and placed too much faith in the results of public opinion polls. In her Ph.D. dissertation on Barkley's later life, Polly Ann Davis concluded that the Kentuckian's most important role in the campaign was to raise enough optimism for party workers to ignore the negative predictions—apparently so did the voters. When the November election tally was complete not only did Truman and Barkley beat the Republican ticket by two million votes but also the Democrats secured control over both houses of Congress. Most newspapers had thought the Democrats would lose, and in a famous blooper the *Chicago Tribune* actually published an edition headlined "Dewey Defeats Truman." A sign on the Washington Post Building caught Barkley's eye after he returned to the capital on November 5, "Welcome Home from the Crow Eaters."

Even before the shock of defeat had been fully absorbed by GOP politicians, a number of leading Republicans bowed to Barkley's qualities and acknowledged the efficacy of the Truman-Barkley ticket in engineering the biggest upset ever experienced in presidential elections. "I think we underestimated," Taft told Barkley on November 6, "the effect of general prosperity, particularly on the farmer and the housewife. And I have to admit that the fight put up by the President and yourself was the final determining factor." The plaudits Barkley received from the opposition continued when he reentered the Senate to complete his last few weeks as a member of Congress. Arthur H. Vandenberg, Michigan's Republican senator and the Senate's president pro tempore, spoke warmly and humorously on the change in status Barkley would soon undergo. "As a result of the recent accident," Vandenberg stated with a devilish twinkle in his eye, "the distinguished senior senator from Kentucky will soon lose his right to stand upon this floor and be recognized. . . . The president pro tempore, with great emphasis on the Latin part of that title, would like to say to the senator from Kentucky—and he knows he speaks for the entire body—that though he may lack the right of recognition on the floor, many other recognitions can never be taken from him. There will always be the recognition of the fact that he is one of the great senators of his time and generation."

On January 20, 1949, Barkley stopped being a senator when fellow Kentuckian and Supreme Court Associate Justice Stanley F. Reed administered the oath of office that converted Barkley into the nation's thirty-fifth vice president. He was proud of the honor bestowed on him by his party's nomination and the people's votes, though he never made a fuss over the additional distinction that he was also the oldest man to enter into these duties. However, coping with obscurity, not age, had been the prerequisite of office before Barkley walked onto the stage. The vice presidency had been the source of political mirth since the time of the Constitutional Convention when Benjamin Franklin suggested the title "Your Superfluous Highness" for the post. "It's a dull job," Vice President Charles Dawes warned Barkley back in 1928. "Every morning you read the papers to ascertain the state of the President's health. Then you go to the Senate to preside over hours of oratorical bilge, fondle your gavel and watch the clock." In fact, one of Barkley's more famous anecdotes—removed from his repertoire after he became vice president—he told to a friend shortly before the 1948 convention: "There once was a farmer who had two sons. Both boys showed great promise early in life. But the elder son went to sea and the younger son was elected Vice President and neither has been heard from since."

Barkley and many of his contemporaries had good reason to stop joking about the vice presidency after he took the oath of office. Not only did the Kentuckian bring new stature to the position, but the course of the president's life reminded Americans that Truman was the third vice president to move up to the White House in the first forty-five years of the twentieth century. Over the years the vice president had become more than just the Senate's presiding officer and tie-breaker and the president's replacement in time of tragedy. The office permitted its occupant to appoint a few Senate committees, sign congressional resolutions, select five candidates each for the Naval Academy and

West Point, and represent the government on the Smithsonian Institution's Board of Regents.

Barkley's stature and Truman's prudence paved the way for even more important tasks that made Barkley the first working vice president in American history. Truman wanted Barkley's legislative experience made available to the entire executive branch of government and hence insisted on Barkley's presence for each cabinet-level meeting. Also, when a congressional bill created the National Security Council, that important policymaking body included the vice president. Finally, Barkley's national fame and speaking abilities prompted the administration to use the vice president as its principal spokesman. One reporter calculated that in the first eight months of 1949 Barkley traveled across the country to deliver forty major addresses in support of the president's positions. This constant visibility in the national limelight turned Barkley's joke about the vice presidency on its ear and led George E. Allen, sometime politician and full-time storyteller, to remark: "Any Vice President who can make the country remember his name and face well enough to keep his identity from becoming a catch question in the radio quiz programs a few weeks after election day is no ordinary man."

Recognizing that Barkley brought extraordinary qualities to his post, President Truman ordered the Heraldic Branch of the Department of the Army to design a special seal and flag for the Office of the Vice President. When the items were finished Truman sent them on to Barkley with the following cryptic note: "I think they are beauties. You can make them step aside now." These prestigious symbols, however, were not nearly so endearing as the title Barkley and his family gave to the office. One evening in the spring of 1949 he spent a quiet time with daughter Marian and grandson Stephen Truitt. The conversation turned to the awkward address, "Mr. Vice President," people used when they met Barkley. Ten-year-old Stephen thought "Gramps" should insert two "e's" between the initials V.P. to form Veep. At his next news conference the proud grandfather told this story and the reporters picked up and began to employ the title of Veep when they wrote articles about the vice president. Unlike the symbols of office created by the Heraldic Branch, Barkley did not pass this label on to his successors. The "Veep" became a special sign for Barkley alone and one that would be used with affection then and thereafter.

As if Barkley had not broken enough new ground to alter permanently the importance and style of the vice presidency, he added one other first. On July 8, 1949, he attended a party given by the Clark Cliffords on board the White House yacht, "Margy." One of the guests, Jane Rucker Hadley, caught the attentions and later the affections of the Veep. Mrs. Hadley, vivacious, attractive, and charming, was the middle-aged widow of a Saint Louis attorney and a secretary for the Wabash Railroad. She had come to Washington for a brief vacation with her close friends, the Cliffords. The moonlit night and the strains of "Some Enchanted Evening" struck a romantic chord in the hearts of Jane and the Veep. Although Jane returned to Saint Louis, Barkley's affinity for planes allowed him to woo her in a cross-country romance that every American faithfully followed in the daily press. "I remember," Secretary of State Dean Acheson later wrote, "the Chief Justice of the United States, Fred Vinson, also of Kentucky, remarking at its height, that between Alben's love affair and Pinza's singing 'Some Enchanted Evening,' Fred could not be sure whether he himself was sixty or sixteen." This whirlwind courtship though not their love affair ended on November 18, 1949, when Alben and Jane shared marriage vows in a simple ceremony before close friends and relatives. Thus Barkley was the first vice president to wed while he held that office.

Not all the accomplishments and activities Barkley undertook as vice president acquired the sympathetic interest of the nation that his romance and marriage raised. In his traditional and constitutional function as the Senate's presiding officer, the Veep more than once engaged in controversies that mirrored beliefs and principles he had long held and also shared with the administration. On October 4, 1949, the Veep voted to break a tie that permitted a farm bill amendment to pass the Senate. The amendment, criticized by several of Barkley's dearest colleagues, allowed farmers 90 percent parity for corn, cotton, peanuts, rice, and wheat. Even though he temporarily lost some friends, Barkley's childhood memories and campaign promises obligated him to break the tie in favor of the amendment.

The most publicly disputed act Barkley performed occurred in March of the same year. He ruled on a motion to end a ten-day filibuster conducted by southern senators who opposed a civil rights bill then being considered. Technically the motion, not the legislation, caused a bitter debate, and both sides had quoted Barkley extensively to buttress their views. The Veep's decision on the motion placed him squarely on the side of those legislators who strove to implement civil rights, but before he presented his emotion-packed ruling he led off with an anecdote. "The Chair," Barkley said, "feels somewhat like the man who was being ridden out of town on a rail. Someone asked him how he liked it. He said if it weren't for the honor of the thing, he would just as soon walk."

Barkley's peers marked his ruling as scurrilous or statesmanlike depending on their position, but few senators could sustain any genuine hatred for a man who so deftly encapsulated a potentially distasteful ruling in a syrup of digestible humor. Fortunately, for the Veep's emotional stability most of his chores in the Senate could be quietly performed or tactfully and wittily fulfilled without arousing the rancor that occurred over the civil rights motion. Congress responded to Barkley's masterful charm by awarding him a special gold medallion for his service, and on March 1, 1951, the thirty-eighth anniversary of his first year in Congress, President Truman made a surprise visit to the Senate chamber to honor the Veep. Truman carried a unique gavel for the Senate's president, a gavel fashioned from the ancient timbers of the renovated White House. In accepting Truman's special gift, Barkley recalled that his early teachers had encouraged him to dream of one day becoming the nation's president. "I have," the Veep admitted, "disappointed those teachers; I have not made the White House; I have not been able to enter it in the capacity in which they predicted I would. So it is very gracious and thoughtful of you to bring a part of the White House to me."

Despite Barkley's implicit concession that the White House was beyond his grasp, he had not yet given up all hope of moving up one final notch on the ladder of his life. Time, though, had become his principal opponent. His age, not the feelings of his heart, worked at cross-purposes with his aspirations. He would not succeed in winning a presidential nomination, but the Iron Man of politics would prove to contemporaries that he kept enough mettle to try, and, when he failed, he still maintained sufficient strength, physical and political, to make a comeback in the arena he knew best.

7

IRON MAN OF POLITICS

THE ANNUAL JEFFERSON-JACKSON Day dinner was held in Washington's National Guard Armory on March 28, 1952. Over a thousand guests occupied more than a hundred tables in a space of coliseumlike dimensions. After dinner, a slight intermission followed which allowed time for a respite before the onslaught of speeches. When the crowd quieted, two men at opposite ends of the room stood up and slowly walked to the middle of the Armory. As Alben W. Barkley and Harry S. Truman met and shook hands the applause that greeted this dramatic gesture reached deafening proportions. The appearance of the president and his Veep had been the prime drawing card for many of those in attendance. They had come in the expectation of seeing Truman and Barkley and they were not disappointed. But the unexpected, at least for one individual, did occur. Truman, half-whispering and half-shouting over the commotion, told Barkley something that caused an expression of surprise to fall across the Veep's face. The president chose that particular moment to tell the vice president that he would not seek his party's nomination at the forthcoming Democratic National Convention.

Later in the evening when Truman spoke he shared with the audience the news he had given to Barkley. Apparently the president had simply tired of the responsibilities and headaches that accompanied his job. In June 1950 he had led the United States and United Nations in a limited and hence controversial war to protect South Korea from conquest by communist North Korea and her allies, the People's Republic of China and the Union of Soviet Socialist Republics. Because the president had to dampen American hopes for a clear-cut victory (and had to fire his principal general, Douglas MacArthur, in the process), his administration had come under increasing attack by right-wing critics such as Republican Senator Joseph R. McCarthy for being "soft" on communism at home. Regardless of Truman's motives, his announcement cleared the way for a wide-open battle among Democratic contenders for the nomination. Exactly two months later, May 28, at the urging of his numerous kind friends Barkley declared his availability for the office he had always wanted. "While I am not," Barkley's statement began, "a candidate in the sense that I am actively seeking the nomination, I have never dodged a responsibility, shirked a duty, or ignored an opportunity to serve the American people. Therefore, if the forthcoming Chicago convention should choose me to lead the fight in the approaching campaign, I would accept."

If Jane Barkley thought the whirl of Washington life almost impossible to absorb, she received quite a jolt when her husband's announcement converted their normally peaceful Kentucky residence, Angles, into a twelve-room beehive of activity from constant visitors and telephone callers. Politicians dropped by or phoned to give their good wishes or advice to Alben in the few weeks between May 28 and the convention's opening day. The news appeared to be universally good. Kentucky's delegates pledged their votes to the favorite son. Barkley's distant cousin and strongest competition, Adlai Stevenson, apparently had decided not to run but instead to seek reelection as governor of Illinois. Finally, President Truman urged his state's delegation to vote for Barkley. Thus Alben became Truman's heir apparent and the administration's handpicked successor.

While Barkley accumulated bits and pieces of positive signs, he rose in a balloon of giddy expectations that could be deflated with the prick of a pin made sharp by somber reality. Strong contenders such as Estes Kefauver and Richard Russell had not abandoned the field of battle to Barkley. Even Stevenson's shadowy figure seemed poised on the brink of materializing at the proper moment. The Illinois governor's on-again, off-again position over the nomination should have been a flashing danger signal to the Barkley camp. But then the "Barkley camp" is a misnomer. The word *camp* evokes a military image of disciplined men in ranks and regiments led by officers in a chain of command. Barkley, however, neglected to marshal and nurture his forces, in part because he failed to articulate clearly his desire to secure his party's endorsement. Hence Barkley's "camp" forgot to count noses and line up the votes of state delegations. The so-called strategy planned by the "camp" would have allowed Kefauver and Russell to knock each other out in the early rounds so that the Veep, like a Phoenix, could emerge victorious on a later ballot.

If Barkley left too much to chance and naively redefined the art of politics, he knew full well the most formidable obstacle across his path to the White House. The previous fall he had gone to Korea and visited American troops. During a stop for a meal on a snow-clad mountain above the Thirty-eighth Parallel, he celebrated his seventy-fourth birthday. No major political party had ever put forward a man his age as its presidential nominee. Barkley was blessed with robust health, but he had suffered a "tired heart" after campaigning strenuously for the party in the 1950 congressional elections. Newspaper reporters who generally and genuinely loved the man had to mention these salient points in background articles on the Veep. And, as much as he tried to minimize or hide his failing eyesight, by 1952 Barkley received information from his seven morning newspapers from Jane, who read to him.

Courageously the man from Paducah decided to confront the issue and confute his critics. On a sweltering Friday, July 18, the Barkleys arrived in Chicago. A barrage of reporters and a motorcade met them for the half-mile trip from the station to the hotel. Disdaining the use of transportation and whispering "This is it!" into Jane's ear, Alben proceeded to walk to the hotel. Photographers, reporters, and Jane had to walk in a half-trot in order to keep up with his brisk pace. Amiably chatting with members of this perspiring retinue, Alben arrived at the hotel convinced he had answered the question of whether he was too old for the White House.

This magnificent act of near bravado was irretrievably upstaged by what occurred Sunday evening before the convention's opening day. Prominent members of the labor movement, led by United Auto Workers President Walter Reuther, issued a statement to the press. It seemed that labor wanted a younger man, such as Stevenson, to be the Democratic nominee. At point-blank range they fired the shot that Barkley feared the most. Labor called the Kentuckian too old to be a serious candidate for the presidency. Initially Barkley tried to fight this attack from men who knew the Veep had been among the workingman's most ardent friends. He hastily called a breakfast meeting with his detractors on Monday, July 21. Morning-paper headlines "Labor Dumps Barkley" made the affair anticlimactic. No one touched their breakfasts, but the words spoken at that time left in Barkley's mouth a foul taste that would remain with him to his grave. Barkley argued in vain that he was younger than Winston Churchill, that Goethe wrote *Faust* at age eighty-two, and that Oliver Wendell Holmes resigned from the Supreme Court at age ninety-one.

Although Barkley's arguments fell on deaf ears, he received during the day enough calls and telegrams of support, including a telegram from United Mine Workers President John L. Lewis, to sweeten partially the morning's bitter events. However, Barkley understood that his backstairs candidacy had collapsed and in the evening acknowledged this fact when he provided a withdrawal statement for the press. Demonstrating emotional restraint and avoiding justifiable vindictiveness, Barkley magnanimously stated: "If by taking myself out of this race, I have contributed to the progress of the Democratic Party and the future welfare of the United States, and, thereby, have rendered a service to my country, then I am most happy."

Barkley was tempted to pack and immediately leave the convention. But delegates in droves stopped by and warmly expressed their good wishes to the man many called "Mr. Democrat." In addition, the party's National Committee asked him to present his own special address on Wednesday. Barkley agreed but told committee members that if he was going to deliver his swan song he wanted prime time. Thus on the evening of July 23, he presented what became his last major speech before a national convention. The audience knew instinctively they were witnessing a historic occasion and greeted the Kentuckian with a thirty-five-minute demonstration. It was a heart-wrenching half-hour, for "Barkley for President" banners dotted the hall and many of the delegates mistakenly believed that their enthusiastic welcome could reverse Barkley's decision.

Finally, to the accompaniment of "No-No!" yells, the Veep spoke and his first comments repeated his statement that removed him from consideration for the nomination. Barkley did not have time to prepare a speech. Even if he had, his failing eyesight would have prevented his reading it. Nevertheless, partly to scotch this spontaneous revival of his candidacy, Barkley decided to begin his impromptu remarks with an anecdote. He told the story of a farmer who went to town in his mule-driven wagon each Saturday night to get drunk. The mules automatically brought the passed-out farmer home, and his sons unhitched the wagon, put the mules in the barn, and carried their father to bed. One Saturday night the sons decided to play a joke by unhitching the mules and leaving their father. The next morning the hung-over farmer awoke and, seeing the muleless wagon tongue, said "I have either lost a damn good pair of mules or I have found a damn good wagon!"

This story was the only veiled reference Barkley made to the "trick" he had suffered at the hands of some labor leaders. Typically, he used this humorous yet poignant way of expressing his resentment without vocally assaulting and permanently antagonizing some members of an important section of the party. Barkley continued his speech by criticizing Republicans and praising his party, but in softer, loftier terms than he had ever used before. Speaking of a "crusade," Barkley hoped that many of the principles he and the party espoused could be continued and extended to bring basic freedom, social justice, and needed peace to the nation and the world. "When that day comes," Barkley concluded, "we shall all rejoice without regard to position, without regard to politics, without regard to race, creed or color, without regard to economic conditions, we will all rejoice in our part in bringing these things to mankind, these things to the world. God grant that it may come in your day and mine. Thank you and goodbye."

As Jane later recalled in her memoirs, *I Married the Veep*, her husband's swan song was a love song for his party, and the audience responded in full measure. Barkley did not receive a simple round of applause. While the band played "My Old Kentucky Home" and Jane came out to raise her hand with Alben's the audience gave the Veep a forty-five-minute ovation, perhaps the longest in convention history. Those minutes, when the party showered Barkley with its warmth and thanks for decades of service, most certainly transformed what might have been an otherwise sad moment into the highlight of Barkley's life. "I think," Truman remarked, "it was the greatest and grandest exit a major withdrawing candidate could make."

Later in the convention's proceedings and without Barkley's knowledge, a member of the Missouri delegation nominated the Veep for president, a motion seconded by House Majority Leader John McCormack. The nomination, however, like the ovation Barkley earlier received merely symbolized the party's affection for the Veep. In actual fact his official withdrawal brought to life and eventual convention victory Stevenson's candidacy for the nomination—which after all may have been the ultimate goal of the "stop Barkley" movement spearheaded by some of the party's labor leaders.

Despite the utter disgust Barkley felt over the way he lost the nomination, he left the convention and moved on to the hustings where he spoke for the Stevenson ticket. The Illinois governor conducted an eloquent and literate campaign, but he could not compete either with Republican themes that criticized Democrats for "Korea, communism, and corruption" or with the popular hero put forward by the GOP, General Dwight D. Eisenhower. In addition, Ike's running mate, California Senator Richard M. Nixon, attacked Stevenson with slogans such as "Adlai the appeaser" and elevated anti-intellectualism to a political creed by describing as an "egghead" the balding Democratic nominee. Finally, Americans answered with a vengeance the old Republican call "Time for a change," when Eisenhower won the popular vote by six million ballots and captured the votes of the electoral college, 442 to 89.

Inauguration Day, January 20, 1953, found Barkley unemployed and without local or national office for the first time in nearly a half-century. Earlier he had personally acknowledged and publicly admitted his need to have his eyes checked. The examination revealed cataracts and shortly after the November election he had undergone the first of two operations to remove the cause of his growing blindness. Regardless of this indication of old age, and although he no longer held office, Barkley remained a public figure and refused to retire. He signed a contract with the National Broadcasting Company to do twenty-six segments of his own television show, "Meet the Veep." The fifteen-minute weekly broadcasts gave Barkley a chance to comment on national events and display his wit in a homey living-room setting. Even though he felt at ease doing the show and counted numerous show-business personalities from comedian Bob Hope to the Grand Ole Opry's Minnie Pearl as his friends, Barkley's "Meet the Veep" did not set a high trend for TV ratings.

NBC did not extend his contract and so in September the Barkleys finally "retired" to Paducah and their Kentucky home, Angles. The Veep, however, continued to be one of the most sought-after speakers in the nation and rarely a week went by that he did not travel to talk to a group of one variety or another in the country. In between trips he arduously worked with journalist Sidney Shalett on his memoirs. Barkley also managed to slim his figure by reducing his craving for quart-sized portions of coffee ice cream and pound-sized snacks of chocolate almonds. Early in 1954 the Iron Man was in fighting trim, positively jittery from "inactivity," and eager to reenter the political arena.

Jane initially objected, but the party openly wanted Barkley to contest the Senate seat then held by Republican John Sherman Cooper. The latter found himself in an unenviable position. Two years earlier he had barely won the right to fill the unexpired term of the deceased Virgil Chapman. Yet Kentucky remained a predominantly Democratic state and as usual in an off-year election votes naturally tend to swing away from the party that controls the White House. When the battle lines were drawn, Kentucky voters had to choose between two similar men both of whom had, in the words of Steven Channing, author of *Kentucky: A Bicentennial History*, "an image of independence and integrity, of concern with large national and even international questions." Even Cooper's biographer, Robert Schulman in *John Sherman Cooper: The Global Kentuckian*, quoted the Republican as saying, "we had trouble finding issues."

Given their similarities, Barkley and Cooper stressed the one remaining issue that kept the men apart, party politics. Thus the visits to Kentucky by such Republican notables as President Eisenhower, Vice President Nixon, and Senator Everett Dirksen only confirmed the direction of Barkley's campaign and undercut the maverick picture Cooper normally projected to Kentucky voters. In essence, Cooper damagingly assumed the GOP mantle in a Democratic state. If these problems were not enough, Cooper took a challenge for his seat from a man determined to erase what had occurred at Chicago and keep his title as the Iron Man of politics. The last six weeks before the November 2 election found Barkley almost frenetically campaigning up and down and across the state in sixteen-hour days that left his wife in a perpetual state of near collapse. Incredibly enough on the last day's canvass on a route that brought the Barkleys home to Paducah, the Veep delivered fifteen speeches—more than par for the grinding pace he had kept for fifty years. Barkley received the vindication he had wanted for the "too old" label. Kentucky voters gave him a plurality of 80,000 votes, a thousand votes, so wags remarked, for each of his years plus 4,000 to grow on.

Two months and a day after the election, January 3, 1955, Barkley walked down the aisle of the Senate chamber. Senior Kentucky Senator Earle C. Clements escorted Kentucky's junior senator-elect to Vice President Nixon, who administered the oath of office. This simple ceremony followed by Barkley's signature on the rolls marked the twelfth time in forty-two years that he entered the nation's service as a legislator. His colleagues and witnesses and members of the gallery spontaneously arose to give him their applause. This small tribute on this occasion meant more to him than many of the memorials he had received. The landscape, for example, around Paducah was dotted with his name and figure, and before long his name would be given to one of the lakes behind the dams on the Tennessee and Cumberland rivers near his home. However, the greatest memorial Barkley built himself. Although he was not an original thinker and possessed an overly uncritical regard for his party, the Iron Man devoted his years to the give-and-take of the democratic process. His life speaks eloquently across generations to inform us that democracy remains a vibrant force as long as sensible individuals can argue the hotly contested issues of the day with the knowledge and wit he displayed. Of all the designations good and bad that friends or critics had attributed to his name, he was proudest of the one that called him "politician."

However, the politician for all his longevity in Congress

had his wings clipped right down to the quills. Not only did he enter the chamber as a junior senator from Kentucky but as for power and seniority he worked from the lowly status of a freshman legislator. A disrupted term of office meant for any returning individual that he or she must start at the back of the line. Barkley, though, accepted gladly the new situation. He turned down Harley Kilgore's offer to exchange with him his front-row seat. The Kentuckian decided he enjoyed his place in the rear of the Senate with those other freshmen who flanked him, Richard Neuberger and Patrick McNamara. While he relished these symbols of a new start that returned for him fond memories of yesteryear, his colleagues could not easily forget that he had been a leader or presiding officer over their affairs. Thus Barkley received an appointment to the prestigious Senate Foreign Relations Committee. In fact, that appointment enabled Barkley to perform a characteristically generous act when he endorsed with his words and votes the selection of his former opponent John Sherman Cooper to the ambassador's post in India. Nevertheless, the senator's back-bench position kept him out of any leadership role and significant involvement with pressing legislative matters.

Time, of course, could cure Barkley's loss of seniority, but time began to run out and in a way he had never expected. Over the winter of 1955-1956 the darkening cloud of growing blindness intruded on Barkley's delightful start to his second career in the Senate. Alben expected quite fully to live a long life. On a lark during one of his trips abroad he went to a palmist who confirmed this happy belief by telling Barkley he could expect to live well into the 1980s. The possibility of blindness never entered the picture Barkley painted of his later years in life. As if to capture and keep the sights he would later miss the Kentuckian enlarged his already busy schedule so he could see those friends and events before their blurred images turned to shadows and then to darkness. In the last few days in April, for example, he addressed the Woodrow Wilson Centennial Dinner, delivered a report to his Senate colleagues, attended an Apple

Blossom Festival in Winchester, Virginia, joined the annual party of the Press Club, helped "Meet the Press" celebrate its tenth anniversary, visited Senator Harry F. Byrd's estate, and, finally, on Monday, April 30, 1956, went to Lexington, Virginia, where he would give a keynote speech for the mock convention conducted by students at Washington and Lee University.

The college students had devoted much serious fun to setting up their own version of a national political convention. Dances, parade preparations, and the refurbishing of the gymnasium had all occurred before the Barkleys arrived for their luncheon engagement with the school's first family, President and Mrs. Francis Gaines. Following the meal Alben took his place in the lead automobile to head a parade of floats through the community. When he completed his part of the route, he returned to the president's home just in time to watch the tail end of the parade and catch an orange tossed by a pretty coed atop the "Florida" float. After a brief rest, Barkley underwent a grilling press conference and then walked to the "convention" to sit with Jane in a front-row seat by the platform.

With the conclusion of introductory ceremonies, the main event began. Barkley was introduced as the keynoter and temporary chairman for the mock convention. Three thousand students gave a rousing welcome to the Kentuckian. He caught this infectious, youthful spirit and sprightly climbed the platform steps to acknowledge the ovation and start his speech. "I have been," Barkley stated after his opening remarks, "temporary chairman of three national conventions, permanent chairman of one, and took part in all of them since 1920. And I have about concluded that . . . I would not go . . . this year. But since arriving in Lexington and since arriving in this hall, the old firehorse hears the bell." The students loved this admission of their effect on his feelings.

The Iron Man continued his speech by outlining the history of Democracy's progress particularly during those years when the speaker played an active part in the story he related. Midway through his recitation he could feel his audience wanted something special and he stopped abruptly and asked directly the students, "You want me to tell you about the fundamentals, don't you?" After a pause the students hesitatingly delivered a "yes." "You don't want me," Barkley proceeded, "to say anything I can't prove, do you?" The students grasped the moment and in an ear-splitting chorus delivered a reverberating "NO!" Barkley had won his audience and held it in his grip. He began to mix his famous anecdotes with inside political stories that kept the students on the edge of their seats with anticipation and laughter.

Near the end of the address Barkley made another quip. This one referred to the parade and the fact he was not a candidate. The Kentuckian had noted that none of the floats had sponsored his name for the nomination before the mock convention. Students yelled "No!" when Barkley stated he was not a candidate for office. "But what," a lone student shouted, "about the old firehorse?" Barkley retorted that he realized motorized equipment had replaced the horse. What he did not know was that the students had planned a special surprise for him. Shortly after his speech a student delegate was to have placed Barkley's name in nomination for the presidency. Apparently ignorant of this pleasant future event Barkley rolled on: "But I have no longer any personal interest. I have served my country and my people for half a century as a Democrat. I went to the House of Representatives in 1913 and served fourteen years. I was a junior Congressman, then I became a senior Congressman, then I went to the Senate and became a junior Senator, and then I became a senior Senator; and then a Majority Leader in the Senate, and then Vice President of the United States, and now I am back again as a junior Senator. And I am willing to be a junior. I'm glad to sit in the back row, for I would rather be a servant in the house of the Lord than sit in the seats of the mighty."

With these words, a résumé of his life that touched the emotions of everyone present, Barkley stepped back and accepted with a bow of his head the deafening ovation. Suddenly, like a shot to his chest, he fell over backwards. Jane rushed to the platform and up the steps. She thought at first he had merely experienced a fainting spell, but it was soon obvious he had suffered a massive and fatal heart attack. The spectacle silenced the crowd which had been so animated by the now lifeless body lying on the platform floor. They were thunderstruck by the suddenness of Barkley's death. But then the Iron Man died as he had lived, working his trade with the effect and strength that made him a most remarkable and durable example of the political man for his and all later generations of Americans.

Sources

MUCH OF THE RESEARCH occurred with the financial assistance provided in a grant from Eastern Kentucky University. The grant permitted me not only to photoduplicate dozens of articles and portions of the manuscript for my various readers but also to travel and do research primarily in the Barkley papers held by Special Collections at the University of Kentucky's King Library. It would be an understatement to describe the Barkley collection as massive. Letters and speeches, movies and tapes, memorabilia and clippings create one of the larger holdings of a prominent historical figure found in this state. However, scholars understand what future Barkley enthusiasts must discover for themselves—a politician's correspondence tends to be as revealing and exciting as watching the pendulum of a grandfather clock. Most of the letters Barkley received are from troubled constituents concerned with their own peculiar problems, and Barkley's replies are diplomatically, if not disappointingly, noncommittal.

Since Barkley was such a significant individual in national politics for such a long time, I have been both blessed and cursed by the abundant material that has been published about the man. A mere compendium composed of each book and article that mentions Barkley's name would require a second volume of a size equal to this tome. Thus in preparing an abbreviated survey of Barkley literature I have had to make an arbitrary decision. Below are discussed or listed only those special works and reflective articles that focus on Barkley. Excluded are popular magazine articles and newspaper stories which would number in multiples of one hundred.

Amazingly enough there are no Barkley biographies. Part of the explanation for this surprising fact lies in the autobiographies written by Alben and Jane. Barkley's *That Reminds Me* (New York, 1954) is a loosely connected collection of his more famous anecdotes that is woven with the aid of journalist Sidney Shalett into Barkley's life history from birth to the end of his term as the Veep. It is a delight to read, but like many autobiographies it tends to gloss over or ignore those events that displease the author. Jane Barkley's *I Married the Veep* (New York, 1958) retells with the help of Frances S. Leighton the May-December love affair carried on by Jane and Alben and fills the gap between Barkley's autobiography and his death. Her highly romantic and now nostalgic book informs us as much or more about Jane as her famous husband.

There are several less accessible but serious studies of Barkley's life. The most complete is George W. Robinson's unpublished manuscript, "Barkley and Roosevelt: A Political Relationship." While the author graciously allowed me to view the fruit of his achievement, Robinson's research is available to a greater audience because portions of the larger manuscript have been published as journal articles: "Alben W. Barkley and the 1944 Tax Veto," *Register of the Kentucky Historical Society* 67 (July 1969): 197-210; "The Making of a Kentucky Senator: Alben W. Barkley and the Gubernatorial Primary of 1923," *Filson Club History Quarterly* 40 (April 1966): 123-35. In addition, two doctoral theses have dealt in some detail with Barkley's career: Polly Ann Davis, "Alben W. Barkley: Senate Majority Leader and Vice President (University of Kentucky, 1963); and Gerald S. Grinde, "The Early Political Career of Alben W. Barkley, 1877-1937" (University of Illinois, 1976). Together these competently accomplished scholarly works provide in three volumes over a thousand pages of narratives, notes, and sources that chronicle every incident associated with Barkley. Part of Grinde's exhaustive and well-written treatise has appeared in print: "Politics and Scandal in the Progressive Era: Alben W. Barkley and the McCracken County

Campaign of 1909," *Filson Club History Quarterly* 50 (April 1976): 36-51. Also, two articles from the Davis study have been published: "Alben W. Barkley's Public Career in 1944," *Filson Club History Quarterly* 51 (April 1977): 143-57; "Alben W. Barkley: Vice President," *Register of the Kentucky Historical Society* 76 (April 1978): 112-32. Barkley's fame as a speaker has justifiably drawn the attentions of two scholars: Charles A. Leistner, "The Political Campaign Speaking of Alben W. Barkley" (Ph.D. diss., University of Missouri, 1958); William R. Mofield, "The Speaking Role of Alben Barkley in the Campaign of 1948" (Ph.D. diss., Southern Illinois University, 1964).

There was not enough space in this brief biographical essay to treat adequately the serious issue of corruption raised by the 1938 campaign. The reader is directed to view John Henry Hatcher, "Alben Barkley, Politics in Relief and the Hatch Act," *Filson Club History Quarterly* 40 (July 1966): 249-64; and note Chandler's response to the Hatcher article in a letter, *Filson Club History Quarterly* 40 (October 1966): 335-37. Ironically, Chandler was charged with using federal funds in his successful bid for the governor post in 1935. However, Robert J. Leupold has virtually exonerated Chandler in "The Kentucky WPA: Relief and Politics, May-November 1935," *Filson Club History Quarterly* 49 (April 1975): 152-68. Unfortunately, I suspect electoral improprieties committed in the 1930s by both Barkley and Chandler organizations (though not necessarily Barkley and Chandler themselves) require further investigation. Finally, Barkley's speeches in Congress are available in the appropriate volumes of the *Congressional Record*, but the Iron Man also took pen in hand and wrote two articles: "Accustomed as I Am to Public Speaking . . .," *Collier's* 127 (June 9, 1951): 20-21, 66; "Why I Support Roosevelt," *Collier's* 118 (May 20, 1944): 11, 92-93.